MacIver, Susanna

Cookery and Pastry

ISBN: 978-1-948837-24-8

This classic reprint was produced from digital files in the Google Books digital collection, which may be found at http://www.books.google.com. The artwork used on the cover is from Wikimedia Commons and remains in the public domain. Omissions and/or errors in this book are due to either the physical condition of the original book or due to the scanning process by Google or its agents.

This edition of Susanna MacIver's **Cookery and Pastry** was originally published in 1789 (London).

Townsends
PO Box 415, Pierceton, IN 46562
www.Townsends.us

COOKERY

AND

PASTRY,

AS TAUGHT AND PRACTISED BY

Mrs MACIVER,

TEACHER OF THOSE ARTS IN EDINBURGH.

A NEW EDITION, WITH ADDITIONS.

TO WHICH ARE ADDED,

FIGURES OF DINNER AND SUPPER COURSES, FROM FIVE TO FIFTEEN DISHES,

A L S O,

A CORRECT LIST OF EVERY THING IN SEASON
FOR EVERY MONTH IN THE YEAR.

LONDON

Printed for C. ELLIOT and T. KAY,
opposite Somerset-Place, Strand; and
C. ELLIOT, Edinburgh.
M,DCC,LXXXIX.

ADVERTISEMENT

TO THE

FORMER EDITIONS.

THE Author's fituation in life hath led her to be much converfant in Cookery, Paftry, &c. and afforded her ample opportunity of knowing the moft approved methods practifed by others, and alfo of making experiments of her own. Some years ago fhe opened a fchool in this city for inftructing young Ladies in this neceffary branch of female education; and fhe hath the fatisfaction to find that fuccefs hath accompanied her labours. And many of her fcholars, and others, having repeatedly folicited her to make her receipts public; thefe folicitations, joined to an hearty defire of doing every thing that it was thought could be ufeful in the way of her bufinefs, have at length determined her to this publication. She is far from thinking this little Book perfect; but as all the receipts contained in it have been frequently practifed by her, fhe is hopeful it will be found a good practical treatife.

Edinburgh, November, 1783.

ADVERTISEMENT

TO

THIS EDITION.

IT was fuggefted by fome friends, that the addition of fome Figures of Courfes for Dinners and Suppers fhould be fubjoined; accordingly, I have made out feveral Courfes from five to fifteen difhes. As for Supper courfes, a lift of things for that purpofe is given, from which any Lady of the fmalleft experience may form Suppers of any extent according to the articles that are in feafon. All the difhes for both Dinners and Suppers are to be found in this little Book; and it is prefumed it is calculated for the genteel and middling ranks of life, and not filled with difhes that will never be ufed by one out of an hundred families that may purchafe them. There is likewife added a correct lift of every thing in Seafon in every month of the year, which will be found particularly ufeful to young houfe-keepers.

SUSANNA MACIVER.

Edinburgh, Dec. 1788.

CONTENTS

CONTENTS.

CHAP. I.

SOUPS.

A ftock for foups or fauces	Page 13
Spices proper to be mixed with any kind of feafoning	14
Imperial white foup	14
Pigeon foup	15
Hare foup	16
Green fummer foup	17
Plumb pottage	17
Leek foup	18
Onion foup	19
Peafe foup	20
To make the fame foup pafs in fummer as green peafe foup	21
Green meagre foup	22

CHAP. II.

FISH.

To drefs a cod's head	22
To roaft a cod's head	23
To broil cod	24
To drefs fmall cod with ale fauce	24
To crimp cod after the Dutch manner	25
To ftew foles	25
To fry foles	26
To roaft falmon	26
To crimp fkate	27
To pot any fort of fifh	27
To pickle oyfters	28
To pickle mufcles or cockles	28
To fricafee oyfters, cockles or mufcles,	29
To ftollop oyfters	30
To brown oyfters in their own juice	30
To drefs haddocks with a brown fauce	31
To ftuff large haddocks	32
To drefs whitens with a white fauce	33
To make parton or crab pies	34
A fricafee of lobfters	35
To ftew trouts with brown fauce	36
To pot eels	36
The beft way of potting frefh herrings	37
To fry turbot	38
To drefs a fea-cat	38
To drefs a fea-cat with a white fauce	39

A 3

CHAP.

CHAP. III.

FLESH.

	Page
To red a rump of beef	40
To make a mutton ham	40
a bacon ham	41
To cure neats tongues	42
To make forced-meat balls	43
To stew a rump of beef	43
a rump of beef with roots	45
Beef a-la-mode,	46
To pot beef	47
To make minced collops	48
To pot a cow's head	49
To broil beef steaks	50
To make Scots (or stewed) beef collops	50
To make beef collops	51
To collar beef	52
Scarlet beef	53
To stew a fillet of veal	53
To make Scotch collops (veal)	54
To hash cold veal	55
To mince cold veal	55
To make veal cutlets	56
Broiled veal cutlets	56
To fricasee a breast of veal	57
To make veal fricandoes	58
veal olives	59
To dress a calf's head	59
To make brain cakes	61
To turtle a calf's head	61
To pot a calf's head	61
To make mutton cutlets	64
To hash cold mutton	64
To make a hancot of mutton	65
To dress a dish of mutton with paper in place of coals	66
To boil a leg of lamb with cabbage or cauliflower	67
Lamb covered with rice	67
To dress a lamb's head	68
chickens with pease and lettuce	70
To make veal or lamb toasts	71
A jugged hare	71
A good Scotch haggies	72
A lamb's haggies	73
A pudding of lamb's blood	74
To make puddings either of sheep or cow's blood	75
liver puddings	75
apple puddings	76

To

CONTENTS.

To make rice puddings   Page 76
     almond puddings in skins   77
To roast a calf's or lamb's liver   77
To ragoo a liver   77
To make cake-jelly of calves feet   78
     portable soup   79
To ragoo pallets and kernels   81
Hare collops   82
To roast a hare   82
To smother rabbits   83
To make a caparata   83
General rules for boiling fowls   84
A parsley sauce   85
An oyster sauce   85
A celery sauce   85
A cream sauce   86
To boil beef or mutton in the juice   86
To roast any piece of venison   87
To stew venison   87
Venison in the blood   88
To stew venison that has been roasted   88
To broil venison   89
To boil a haunch of venison   89
To roast and stuff a turkey   89
The best sauce for a roasted hen   90
To roast a goose or duck   91
To dress a wild duck   91
To ragoo a pair of ducks   92
To make a tame duck pass for a wild one   93
To pot geese the French way   93
A general rule for roasting wild-fowl   94
To pot any kind of wild-fowl   95
     pigeons   95
To stove pigeons   96
To ragoo pigeons   97
To broil pigeons whole   98
Disguised pigeons   99
A pigeon dumpling   99
To stew cold roasted wild-fowl or hare   100
To ragoo rabbits   101
To stew a neat's tongue whole   101
To hash a cold neat's tongue   102
A sauce for a roasted tongue   103
To potch eggs with sorrel   103
An aumulette   104
Egg and onions, commonly called the onion dish   105

CHAP.

CHAP. IV.

PIES, PASTIES, &c.

To make a beef-steak pie — — Page 105
a mutton-steak pie 106
a venison pasty 106
A mock venison pasty — 107
To make a veal florentine — 108
a pigeon pie 109
a chicken pie 109
superfine minced pies 110
a common minced pie 111
a giblet pie 112
a hare or moorfowl pie 113
a kernel pie 113
a calf's-foot pie 114
A marrow pasty 115
An egg pie 115
An eel pie 116
A cad florentine 116
An apple pie 117
An apple pie with potatoes 117
A chefnut pie 118
A gooseberry pie 118
To make puffed paste 119
A common pie paste 119
To make paste for the cases of preserved tarts 120
A paste for raised pies 121
To make apple tarts 121
Gooseberry tarts 122
Cherry tarts 122
To make rasberry or currant tarts 122
prune tarts 123
Peach or apricot tarts 123
To make a glazing for tarts 124
A light boil'd pudding 124
A boil'd custard pudding 125
A plumb pudding 125
A plain suet pudding 126
A boiled bread pudding 126
A boiled rice pudding 127
A pease pudding 128
A whole rice pudding 128
Another rice pudding 129
A lair pudding 129
A marrow pudding 130
A tansy pudding 131

CONTENTS.

An orange pudding - - Page 132
A lemon pudding - - - 133
A citron pudding - - - 133
A green gooseberry pudding - - 134
An apple pudding - - - 135
An almond pudding - - - 135
A sago or millet pudding - - 136
A potatoe pudding - 136
A common potatoe pudding to be fired below roasted meat 137
A bread pudding to be fired below meat - 138
A hasty pudding - - 138
A carrot pudding - - 139
An apple dumpling - 140
Sir Robert Walpole's dumplings - 141
To make curd cheese-cakes - - 142
 lemon cheese-cakes - - 143
 almond cheese-cakes - - 143
 custards - - 144
 rice custards - - 144
 almond custards - - 145
 clear lemon cream - - 146
 an orange cream - 146
 ratafia cream - - 147
 sweet almond cream - - 148
 clouted cream - - 148
 velvet cream - - 149
 steeple cream - - 149
 bandstring curd - - 150
Rush curd - - 150
Tender curd - - 151
To make fair butter - - 152
Syllabubs - - - 152
Another kind of syllabubs - 153
Blanc-marge - - 153
Gooseberry cream - - 154
To make strawberry, rasberry, or currant cream 155
To make rice cream - 155
A rich eating posset - 156
A common eating posset - 157
To make hartshorn jelly - 157
Calves-feet jelly - 158
Jelly for a consumption - 159
A hen's nest - - 160
Jelly in cream - - 160
To dish up cold chicken in jelly - 161
A floating island - 162
A trifle - 162

CONTENTS.

An egg cheefe   Page 164
To make a cheefe loaf   164
     fine pancakes   165
     a very good baked pudding with the fame batter   166
To turn the fame batter into a different form   167
To make pan-puddings   167
     apple fritters   168
     currant fritters   169
     oyfter fritters   169
     potatoe fritters   170
     a tanfy cake   170
The poor knights of Windfor   171
To make fmall curd puddings   172
     a curd florentine   173
To ftew parfnips   173
     red cabbage   174
     cucumbers   174
To drefs parfnips to eat like fkirrets   175
Celery with cream   176
To ftew celery in gravy   176
To have a difh of kidney-beans in the winter   177
To keep artichoke bottoms the whole year   178
The beft way of keeping green goofeberries for tarts   179
To make white cuftards   180
     German puffs   181
     apple puffs   181
     fhort-bread   182
     a rich bun   183
     a fourthpart plumb-cake   185
     a feed-cake   186
     a diet-loaf   187
     a currant-cake   187
To make fine ginger-bread   188
     common bifcuit   189
     the fame bifcuit proper for beating to put in fine
       puddings   189
To make Savoy bifcuit   189
     fpunge bifcuit   190
     common almond bifcuit   190
     ratafia drops   191
     fquirt, fruit, and fhaving bifcuit   191

CHAP. V.

PRESERVES, PICKLES, &c.

To clarify fugar   193
To make fmooth marmalade   194

To

CONTENTS.

To make chip marmalade   Page 195
To preserve whole oranges   196
  orange skins   198
Preserved sliced oranges   199
To preserve orange grate   201
Orange chips   202
To make orange-peel   202
To candy angelica   203
  flowers   204
To make red-currant jelly   205
White-currant jelly   206
Black-currant jelly   206
To preserve whole currants   208
An excellent way of doing currants for present use   209
To preserve rasberries whole   210
To make rasberry jam   211
To preserve green goofeberries   211
  red goofeberries   213
To make goofeberry jam   214
  goofeberry jelly   214
To preserve cherries   215
  cherries with stalks and leaves   216
  apricots   217
To make apricot jam   218
To preserve green gauge plums   218
  magnum plums   220
To keep common plums for tarts   221
To preserve peaches   221
  pears   222
  pears red   222
To make apple jelly   223
Chip and jelly of apples   224
To preserve apples green   225
Apples in fyrup   227
To preserve cucumbers   227
  melons   230
  green almonds   230
  barberries   231
To make lemon fyrup   232
Syrup of clove julyflower   233
  of violets   234
  of pale rofes   234
  of maidenhair   235
  of turnip   235
  of nettles   236
Conferve of rofes   236
To make tablets   237
To

To make barley-fugar - - Page 238
      glazing for feed or plum-cake - 239
To mango cucumbers - - - 239
To pickle walnuts - - - 241
      mufhrooms - - 242
      Cauliflowers . - -- 243
      onions - - - 244
      red cabbage - - 244
      beet-root - - 245
      barberries - - 246
To make pickle-lillo, or Indian pickle - 246
      fugar vinegar - - 248
      goofeberry vinegar - 248
      ketchup - - 249
      walnut ketchup - - 249
      a twenty-pint barrel of double-rum fhrub 251
      the true French white ratafia - 251
Family dinners of five difhes - - 253
      feven difhes - - 254
      eight difhes - .- 255
      nine difhes - - 255
      ten difhes· - - 256
      twelve difhes - · 256
      fifteen difhes - 256
Things for fupper difhes - - 257
Lift of things in feafon in every month of the year 258

N. B. The liquid measure is given in Scotch : but it can in a minute be reduced into Englifh by the following :

    Englifh and Scotch gallon (wine and fpirit meafure) the fame ;

    1 Scotch pint is equal to 4 Englifh pints ;

    1 Scotch chepin to 2 Englifh pints ;

    1 Scoth mutchkin to one Englifh pint ;

    1 Scotch half-mutchkin to a half-pint Englifh ; and fo on.

COOKERY

COOKERY AND PASTRY.

CHAP. I.

SOUPS.

A Stock for Soups or Sauces.

TAKE a round of beef and put it
into a pot of cold water. If it is
a large piece, let it boil three quarters
of an hour. Take it out, and fcore it
well on all fides with a knife, to draw
the juice from it; then put the beef and
juice into the pot again; put in fome
whole black and Jamaica pepper, a few
cloves, a faggot of fweet herbs, two or
three onions, and a large carrot. Let
all boil together, until the whole fubftance is out of the meat; then ftrain it
off, and let it ftand all night; take off
all the fat, then pour it off from the
grounds.

grounds. This is an excellent soup, or a fine stock for any rich sauces. If you want the soup brown, put in a little black crust of a fine loaf, and a few onion skins, along with the rest of the seasonings : dish it up on toasted bread ; and, if you please, put in about two ounces of vermicelli.

Spices,

Proper to be mixed with any kind of seasoning.

Take an ounce of black and an ounce of Jamaica pepper, two drop of cloves, and two or three nutmegs ; beat them into a powder, and mix them all together, and put them in a box or bottle, so as they catch no air ; and then you have them ready for seasoning any kind of sauce.

Imperial White Soup.

Take three or four pound of a round of beef, blanch it all night in cold water ; put it on the fire in a pot of cold water alongst with a gigot of lamb ;

put

put in fome whole white pepper, a few
cloves, and a blade of mace ; tie up a
faggot of parſley and chives*, or young
onions. Let all boil till the ſubſtance
is entirely out of the meat ; then ſtrain
it off, and put in as much ſweet cream
as will make it white, and ſalt to your
taſte ; put it on the fire to warm, and
diſh it up on toaſted bread,

Pigeon Soup.

Take eight good pigeons, take the
pinions, necks, gizzards, and livers ;
cut down two of the worſt of the pigeons, and put them on with as much
water as will make a large diſh of ſoup;
boil them till all the ſubſtance is out
of them ; then ſtrain them off ; ſeaſon
the whole pigeons within with your
mixed ſpices and ſalt ; truſs them with
their legs into their belly ; take a large
handful of parſley, chives or young
onions, and a good deal of ſpinage ;
pick and waſh the herbs very clean ;
                                    ſhred

Chives are what the country people call Scythes.

fhred them, but not too fmall; take
about a handful of grated bread, put a
good piece of butter in a frying-pan,
let it come to boil, and then throw in
the bread amongft the boiling butter,
clófe ftirring the bread from the bottom
of the pan with a knife, until it becomes
of a fine brown colour. Then put on
your ftock to boil, and then put in the
whole pigeons alongft with the herbs
and fried bread; and let them boil together till the pigeons are enough done,
and then difh them up with the foup.
If you do not find the foup enough feafoned, put in a little more of the mixed
fpices and falt.

Hare Soup.

Take a hare, cut it down, wafh it
through two or three waters very well,
fave all the blood, and break the clots
in the wafhings; then run it through a
fearce; put on all the wafhings and
blood with a good piece of lean beef.
Let thefe boil together a good time before you put in the hare; feafon it with
falt

falt and mixed fpices, a faggot of fweet
herbs, and two or three onions; thicken
it with a little browned butter and
flour.   Some like it with a few currants in it; but this is as you choofe.
Then difh it up (after taking out the
herbs and onions) altogether.

Green Summer Soup.

Take as much of the ftock of beef as
will make a good difh of foup; take
the fame herbs and fried crumb of
bread, and order them all in the fame
manner as in the pigeon foup; parboil
a carrot or two, and cut them very fmall;
take fome young green peafe, then put
in the carrots and peafe along with the
reft of the herbs.   If you have not the
ftock of beef, cut down the back-ribs of
mutton, and put it in as you do in common hotchpotch, and difh it up in the
fame way.

Plumb Pottage.

Take a hough of beef and a knuckle
of veal; put them on the fire in a clofs

B 2   pot,

pot, with fix or feven Scots pints (three
and a half gallons) of water; take out the
veal before it is over boiled, and let the
beef boil till the whole fubftance is out of
it; ftrain off the ftock, and put in the
crumb of a twopenny loaf, two pounds
of currants well cleaned, two pounds of
raifins ftoned, and one pound of prunes.
Let all boil together till they fwell; then
warm the veal, and put it in the middle
of the difh.

Leek Soup.

Take large leeks, according to the difh
you intend; cut them about an inch
long, with as much of the tender green
as you can; throw them into water as
you cut them; then cut fome flices of
bread, neither too thick nor too thin;
put in fome butter into a frying-pan;
when it boils, cut the bread into fquare
pieces, lay them in, and brown them
on both fides; have fome prunes ready
wafhed; if they are dry, take the leeks
out of the firft water, and wafh them
through another; have as much water
boiling

boiling in a pan as will cover your materials; throw them all into it, and feafon it with falt and mixed fpices. When the leeks are enough done, your foup is ready.

Onion Soup.

Take half a pound of fplit peafe, which put into two pints of water (one gallon); let them boil till the peafe are diffolved; ftrain them off; take half a pound of butter, put it in a ftew-pan, and boil it until it have done with making a noife; take ten onions, cut them fmall, and throw them into the butter; fry them a little, then drudge fome flour on them, ftirring them all the time: let them fry a little after: then pour your ftock boiling hot on them, and let them boil a little time; then ftrain it off again, put in a few whole fmall onions, paired or fkinned, into your foup, and boil them until they are enough done; feafon it with mixed fpices and falt to your tafte; diſh it up on fried bread, and tha whole onions.

Peafe

Peafe Soup.

Take a pound of fplit peafe ; put them in cold water, with a piece of butter, a large leek or an onion or two, and a large parfnip or carrot; let all boil until the peafe are diffolved ; turn them into a drainer, and bruife the peafe with the back of a fpoon ; then put in fome of the thin, till the peafe are quite wafhed through the drainer; then turn it back into the pot, and let it boil ; then feafon it with falt and mixed fpices. If you want it to look green, beat fome fpinage, and fqueeze out the juice, which put into the foup, with a handful of fpinage-leaves. When this is boiled enough, the foup is ready. Difh it on fried bread. If you choofe fweet herbs, you may throw in a fprig of thyme, winter-favory, and mint, into the ftock ; likewife a red herring, if you choofe it. Some choofe a piece of pork, hung bacon, or a piece of beef ; in either of thefe cafes, put no butter in

your

your ſtock.   Diſh up the meat in your
ſoup.

To make the ſame Soup paſs in Summer as
Green Peaſe Soup.

Take the foregoing ſoup ; and as the
green peaſe are a great deal ſweeter than
the dried peaſe, put in a little ſugar,
and a good deal of the ſpinage-juice;
to make it of a fine green, put in ſome
green peaſe ; and when they are enough.
the ſoup is ready.

Green meagre Soup.

Take ſome celery, two or three carrots, a turnip or two, and half a pound
of ſplit peaſe ; put them all on in boiling water, with a good piece of butter,
and a ſprig of winter-ſavory ; let them
all boil together about an hour and a
half; then ſtrain it off the roots ; take
ſome parſley, ſpinage, chives or young
onions, and chervel ; ſhred them groſs-
ly, and boil them in the ſtock ; thicken
it with fried crumb of bread, and ſea-
son

fon it with your mixed fpices and falt;
then difh it up.

CHAP. II.

F I S H.

To drefs a Cod's Head.

PUT the head and a piece of the
fhoulders into a pan of boiling water; be fure the fifh is covered with the
water, throw in a good deal of falt
and vinegar to make the fauce; take
ftock made either of beef or fifh;
work a good piece of butter and
flour together; ftir it in your fauce
till the butter is melted; then put in
fome pickled oyfters with fome of
their liquor, a lobfter cut in pieces,
a whole onion, the fqueeze of a lemon, and a little of the peel, a little
white-wine ketchup, and mixed fpices
and falt. Let all boil together a little
time;

time ; then throw in a few pickles into
the fauce juft when you are going to
difh it. It ought to be put in a very
deep difh, as it requires a great deal of
fauce. If your difh does not hold it all,
put the remainder in a bowl, and fend
it to the table with the difh. Garnifh
it with fried flounders, fpirlings, or
whitings ; put a little fried parfley between every fifh. If you have no fifhes,
fupply their place with horfe-radifhes
fcrapped.

To roaft a Cod's Head.

Take the head and fhoulders, and lay
it in a flat tin pan ; ftew a little falt
over it ; put it into a quick hot oven
about half an hour ; then take it out,
and pour off all the watery ftuff from
it ; bafte it well with butter, and ftrew
fome mixed fpices over it ; put it into
the oven again for fome time, drawing
it often to the mouth of the oven, and
bafting it with the butter. When you
fee it is enough fired, difh it in the fame
way you do the boiled head, and the
fame

fame fauce; adding thereto two or three
anchovies, if you have them.

To broil Cod.

Cut in pieces about an inch thick;
duft it with flour, and lay it upon the
gridiron over a flow fire. Take a little
gravy, a glafs of white-wine, falt and
fpices, a few pickled oyfters, and a little ketchup, thickening them with a
little butter rolled in flour. Send the
fauce in a difh to table.

To drefs fmall Cod with Ale-fauce.

Put on fome twopenny, or fmall beer;
have fome browned butter ready, thick-
ened with flour; pour it on the ale boiling, keeping ftirring all the while; then
divide the codlings into two or three
pieces, according to their fize; put in
the heads along with them into the
fauce, two or three cut onions, falt and
mixed fpices, fome lemon-peel, and a
little ketchup. Put it in a foup-difh,
with fome cut pickles.

To

To crimp Cod after the Dutch manner.

Boil two pints (one gallon) of water and a pound of falt; fkim it very clean; cut the cod in thin flices; put it into boiling water for three minutes; drain it well from the water; garnifh your difh with parfley. It fhould be eat with oil, muftard, and vinegar.

To ftew Soles.

Skin the foles; flour them; then put them in a panful of brown butter boiling hot; fry them a light brown; then drain all the fat from them; brown a good piece of butter in flour, to which put a little gravy, a few oyfters and their liquor, a bunch of fweet herbs, fome onions, a little claret, the fqueeze of a lemon, and an anchovy; mix them altogether, then put in the foles; let them ftew over a very flow fire half an hour. When you are going to difh the foles (take out the fweet herbs and onions), feafon them with falt and mixed

ed fpices ; garnifh your difh with fliced lemons.

To fry Soles.

Skin and fcore them crofs-ways ; drudge them with flour ; then fry them in a panful of brown butter boiling hot, till they are of a fine brown. Difh and garnifh them with parfley and fliced orange. Beef drippings, when fweet, will anfwer better than butter to fry them with.

To roaft Salmon.

Wafh and fcrape the fcales from it very clean ; dry it with a cloth ; cut it crofs-ways; ftrew it over with falt, mixed fpices, and grated crumbs of bread ; then lay it in a tin pan, putting a little butter in the bottom of the pan, and plenty above the falmon ; put it in the oven till it is enough. It may be eat with oyfter-fauce, or beat butter and parfley. A grilfe done in the oven is a very fine difh. Turn the tail into the mouth, and be fure you do not fcore it

as

as you do the falmon; ftrew falt and mixed fpices over it, with plenty of butter above and below it. Eat it with the fame fauce as the falmon. Garnifh both with parfley.

To crimp Skate.

Cut it about an inch broad; turn each piece round, and tie it with a thread; have as much falt and water ready boiling as will cover it; put it in, and boil it on a very quick fire; cut off the threads, and put it on a dry difh. If you are to eat it hot, fend beat butter and parfley along with it. Garnifh with parfley.

To pot any fort of Fifh.

Scrape and clean them well; cut them in middling pieces; feafon them with falt and fpices; pack them clofe up in a potting-can, with plenty of butter above and below; tie fome folds of coarfe paper on the pot; then put them in a flow oven, and when they are enough fired, take them out of the can, and drain them
well

well from their liquor ; let both cool ;
put the fifh into fmall white pots ; fkim
all the butter off the liquor ; then take
fome more butter along with that you
take from the liquor ; melt it down,
and pour it on the fifh. Send them in
the pots to table.

To pickle Oyſters.

Open the oyfters and throw them into a bafon ; wafh them in their own liquor, and take them out one by one ;
then ftrain the liquor, and let it ftand to
fettle ; you may add a little water to it ;
fet it on the fire to boil ; put a good
deal of whole pepper, fome blades of
mace and nutmeg; let your oyfters have
a boil and keep them ftirring ; when you
think them enough done, take them off,
put them into an earthen pot and cover
them very clofe ; be fure you have liquor enough to cover them ; you may
eat them next day if you pleafe.

To pickle Mufcles or Cockles.

Take your mufcles, beard and wafh
them

them very clean; put them in a pot to
open over the fire; take them out of
their fhells and lay them to cool; put
their liquor into a clean bafon, and let
it ftand till any fand or grit fall to the
bottom; then pour off the clear; take
ginger, mace and black pepper, and
put to your liquor; make it fcalding
hot; put in your cockles or mufcles and
let them ftew a while, and pour them
into a cullender; let them lie till quite
cold and the liquor cold likewife; fo
put them together in a can or jug, and
tie them clofe up, and keep them for
ufe.

To fricafee Oyfters, Cockles, or Mufcles.

Wafh them thoroughly clean in their
own liquour, then ftrain the clean liquor
on them; put them on the fire, and
give them a fcald; lift them out of the
liquor; take fome of the liquor, and
thicken it with a little butter and flour
kned together.   When it comes to boil,
put in the fifh, and let them juft get a
boil or two. Have fome yolks of eggs;

caft

caft two, three, or more, according to the fize of the difh you make; take a little of the liquor out of the pan, and mix it with the yolks of eggs; then put them in the pan, and give them a tofs or two, but don't let them boil; then difh them

To fcallop Oyfters.

Clean and fcald them; put a little butter into your fcallops; fill them with the oyfters; feafon them with a little falt and fpices. As you fill the fcallops, put in a little of the liquor, with half a fpoonful of white-wine. When the fcallops are filled with the oyfters, cover them with crumbs of bread, and lay fmall pieces of butter above all. You may do them in an oven, or brown them before the fire.

To brown Oyfters in their own juice.

Take the largeft you can get: wafh them clean through their own juice; lay them clofe together in a frying-pan, but don't put one above another: make
them

them of a fine brown on both fides ;
if one panful is not fufficient, do off
more ; when they are all done, pour in
fome of their juice into the pan ; let it
boil a little, and mix any of the thicknefs of the oyfters that may remain in
the pan, and then pour it over them.
Of all the ways of dreffing them, this
is the moft delicious.

To drefs Haddocks with a Brown Sauce.

Take the largeft you can get ; clean
them well, and cut off the heads, tails,
belly (or what is commonly called the
lugs), and fins : lay the fifh in as
much fmall ale and vinegar as will cover them ; let them lie in it as long as
you can ; take the heads, tails, &c. and
cut down one of the fifh ; put them all
together in a pan, with as much water
as will be fauce ; put in an onion or
two, a fprig of winter-favory, thyme,
and a little lemon-peel ; let all boil till
the whole fubftance is out of the fifh ;
then ftrain off the ftock. Brown fome
butter, and thicken it with flour ; mix
in

in the ftock with fome ketchup, mixed
fpices, and falt. You may put in a
fpoonful of walnut-pickle, if you have
any. When the fauce comes a-boil,
put in your fifh; have fome oyfters or
mufcles ready, and put either of them
in with a little of their juice; put in
fome cut pickles juft when you are a-
bout to difh them; or if you want your
fauce to be richer, make your ftock of
beef in place of fifh. It is much the
better of a little wine: you may put in
fome claret.

To ftuff large Haddocks.

Open them at the gills, and take
out the guts, but don't flit up the
belly; be fure to clean them well.
Boil fome of them in falt and water;
then fkin and take the bones from
them, and chop them on your mincing board very fmall. If your winter-favory and thyme is dried, beat
and fearch them; feafon the chopped
fifh with falt and mixed fpices. You
muft work them up with a good deal
of

of fweet butter, and as much beat
eggs as will make them ftick; then
ftuff the bellies of your haddocks with
the forc'd meat ; keep fome of it to roll
up in balls ; be fure to fry them in
brown butter; make the fauce the fame
as the former, and boil the fifh in it;
be fure that the fauce cover them : put
in the balls, and give them a boil along
with the fifh. If the fifh have roes, boil
them alone in falt and water; garnifh
the difh with them and parfley. You
muft lay them in ale and vinegar, as in
the former receipt.

To drefs Whitings with a White Sauce.

Clean them well, and lay them in falt
and water. You may make your ftock
of haddocks, or if you pleafe, the broth
of a young cock, and feafon it with falt,
whole white pepper, mace, lemon-peel,
and two or three cloves. When this is
enough, ftrain it off, and turn it back
into the pan, and thicken it with butter wrought in flour. When it boils,
have fome, parfley, chives, or young
                              onions,

onions, minced fmall, and put them in
the fauce; let them boil a little before
you put in whitings, for a very little
will do them ; caft fome yolks of eggs,
according to the fize of the difh; fcrape
a little nutmeg amongft the eggs, a
glafs of white-wine, and a little of the
juice of a lemon ; then take out a little
of the boiling fauce, and mix with the
eggs, pour all into the pan amongft the
fauce, keeping it fhaking over the fire.
Be fure you never let any fauce boil after the eggs go in.   Small haddocks
dreffed the fame way are very good,

To make Parton (Crab) Pies.

After your partons (crabs) are boiled,
pick the meat clean out of the body and
toes (claws); be fure that you leave none
of the fhells amongft the meat; feafon it
with falt and fpices; put in fome crumbs
of bread ; but them in a pan with a
good deal of red or white wine, but
red is preferable ; put in alfo a good
quantity of butter; then put them on
the fire, and let them be thoroughly
boiled;

boiled ; wafh the fhells of the body very clean, and fill them up with the meat, fo far as it will go ; fire them in an o- ven, or, if you have not an oven at hand, put them on a gridiron over a clear fire ; then brown them before the fire.

A Fricafee of Lobfters.

After boiling your lobfters, pick the meat out of the toes (claws) and tail; cut it into fquare or long pieces, not too fmall; pick alfo all the good meat out of the body. If it be a coral lobfter, be fure you take all the red: Take as much good ftock of any kind of meat as will cover them ; in which you may boil a blade of mace and fome lemon-peel ; thicken it with a piece of butter wrought in flour ; when it boils, put in your lob- fters ; caft the eggs and other materials in the fame manner as in the fauce for the whitings : do not have too much fauce, as it muft be pretty thick. All fricafee fauces are the better of a little thick fweet cream. Take fome of the under

under ends of the fmall toes, (claws) and
fliced lemon for garnifhing your difh.

To flew Trouts with Brown Sauce.

After they are cleaned, dry them very
well; duft them with flour, and brown
them a little in the frying-pan; take as
much ftock of either beef or fifh; put
in a faggot of fweet herbs, and an onion
or two; ftrain of your ftock; thicken
it with browned butter and flour; feafon it with fpices, falt, ketchup, a little
walnut-pickle, and fome claret. When
the fauce comes a-boil, put in the trouts,
and ftew them until they be enough. If
you choofe them with a white fauce,
do them in the fame manner as the
whitings. You may drefs pike or eel
in the fame way as the trouts with a
brown fauce, taking care to cut the eels
in pieces about three or four inches
long.

To pot Eels.

After taking the fkin off your eels,
fplit them from the fhoulders to the
tail,

tail, and bone them; feafon them very highly with falt, fpices, and fweet herbs; then put every two together, the infide of the fhoulders of the one to the infide of the tail of the other; roll every pair up as you do a collar, and take as many of them as will fill your potting-can, putting fome butter above and below them : cover them with coarfe paper; put them in the oven, which muft not be too hot; it will be a good while before they be enough. When you difh them, put one of the collars in the middle of the affet (difh), and cut another into thin flices, and put round the one in the middle. You may garnifh them with any green thing you choofe.

Beft way of potting frefh Herrings.

Scale them, and make them very clean; feafon them well with falt and fpices; pack them neatly in your potting-can, laying the fhoulders of the one to the tail of the other. When you have as many in as you intend, pour

on

on as much vinegar as will cover them;
bind them clofe up, and put them in a
flow oven. They will take about four
hours of doing.

To fry Turbot.

Slice the turbot as thin as you can ;
flour them, and fry them on both fides
of a fine brown; beat fome butter; put
a little walnut pickle, fome pickled
oyfters, and a little ketchup in it for a
fauce, which you may pour over the
turbot: garnifh them with fliced lemon or pickles. The tail-cut is the
beft for frying.

To drefs a Sea-cat.

Wafh it very clean, and fkin it; turn
the tail into the mouth ; take fome
good ftock, thicken it with browned
butter and flour; put in fome claret,
ketchup, falt, and fpices, two or three
anchovies, fome pickled oyfters with
fome of their liquor, fome cut pickled
walnuts with a little of their pickle;
be fure to have as much fauce as will
cover

cover the fifh; boil the fifh amongft
the fauce; then difh it, and put the
fauce about it.

To drefs a Sea-cat with a white Sauce.

Order the fifh as in the former receipt; boil it in falt and water; and
for fauce take fome good ftock; thick-
en it with butter; work in flour a little
white-wine, a blade of mace, a little
piece of lemon-peel, an anchovy, fome
pickled oyfters, and a little of their liquor. When the fauce is ready, beat
the yolk of an egg, and mix it with it;
difh it, and pour the fauce over it.

Anchovies, oyfters, pickled walnuts,
and lemon-peel, are fine ingredients
for all kinds of dreffed fifh. If you
have no ftock made of meat, you may
make a very good one of fifh. The
proper fifh for it are haddocks, whitings, and flounders.

C 2   CHAP.

CHAP. III.

F L E S H.

To red a Rump of Beef.

FOR one rump, take two ounces of
faltpetre, a quarter of a pound
brown fugar, half a pound bay falt, one
ounce of Jamaica pepper, two drops of
cloves, a nutmeg or two; beat and
mix them altogether, and rub it into
the beef as well as you can; then rub
it over with common falt; bed and
cover it with the fame; let it lie three
weeks, turning it every other day, and
then hang it up.

To make Mutton Hams.

Half a pound of bay falt, a quarter
of a pound of fugar, will do three or
four mutton hams. If they are very
large, allow half an ounce of faltpetre
to each ham, and the fame fpices as in
the

above receipt. Thrust your finger down
the hole of the shank, and stuff it well
with the salts and spices; rub them
well over with the same; then rub
them over with common salt, and pack
them in the trough, turning them every
other day for a fortnight, and then
hang them up.

To make a Bacon Ham.

Take a pound of common and a pound
of bay salt, two ounces of saltpetre, an
ounce of salprunella, a quarter of a
pound of coarse sugar, and spices as in
the former receipts; mix all well together: open it a little at the shank; stuff
it well with the salt and spices; then tie
it hard up with pack-thread round the
shank-bone to keep the air out of it;
rub it all over with the mixture as well
as possible; lay it in a trough, and strew
a little salt above and below it; take
two or three folds of an old blanket,
and cover the trough to keep out the
air.   After it has lain that way two or
three days, pour off all that brine; then
take

take what was left of the mixed falts,
and mix in fome more common falt
with them: rub the ham every day
with it, turning it, and throwing away
the old brine every day. Continue fo
doing for three weeks; be fure to cover the trough always with the cloth;
lay the ham upon a table, with boards
and weights above it; then hang it up.

All hung-meat is beft fmoked with
wood; juniper is the beft, if you have
it.

To cure Neats Tongues.

Rub them well with common falt,
and let them lie three or four days;
then lay them in a heap on a table to
let the brine run from them; then mix
as much common falt, bay falt, faltpetre, and coarfe fugar, as will do the
quantity of tongues; ftrew fome common falt in the bottom of a barrel; pack
in the tongues neatly, and on every
row of them ftrew the mixed falts; if
you have not enough, make it up with
common falt; put on the finking board
and

and weights above to bring up the
brine to cover them ; then clofe up the
barrel.

To make Forced-meat Balls.

Take the lean part of beef, pork, veal,
or mutton, as much beef-fuet as meat;
mince them fo fmall as they will fpread
on your fingers like pafte ; fpread and
feafon it with mixed fpices and falt ;
work it up with a beat egg to faften it ;
have a little dry flour in the palm of
your hand, and roll them up in balls,
or long-like faufages ; fry them with
browned butter. You may put fweet
herbs in forced meat if you choofe it.

You will get the fifh-forced meat in
the receipt for ftuffing haddocks.

To ftew a Rump of Beef.

Take the big bone out of it ; make
fome holes in it with a knife ; put in
fome mixed fpices and falt in every hole,
and turn your finger round it. If you
choofe to ftuff it, fill up the holes with
forced meat. In that cafe, you need not
C 4   put

put in the falt and fpices in the holes ;
rub the beef over with the falt and fpices ; let it lie a day or two in that feafoning ; take it up the morning it is to
be drefled ; dry it well with a cloth,
and rub it over with beat eggs, and duft
it with flour ; have fome browned butter ready in a frying-pan ; lay in the
beef, and turn it round in the frying-
pan browned over ; have water boiling
in the pot, and put in the beef ; you
muft not have too much about it ; keep
the pot very clofe covered after it is
once come a-boil ; you muft keep it
ftewing over a flow fire, only fimmer-
ing all the while ; turn the beef frequently, as it muft not have too much
liquor about it. If it is a very large
rump, it will take three hours doing ;
take up fome of the broth, fcum all the
fat clean off it ; take forced meat, fome
of it rolled in balls, and fome long like
faufages ; brown them in butter in the
frying-pan : drain all the greafe clean
from them ; have a couple of pallets
ready and fome kernels ; parboil and
brown

brown them a little; have fome truffles
and morals; be fure to fcald them a
little; cut the pallets in fquare pieces.
If the kernels be large, cut them in two
or three pieces; take the ftock that you
took out of the pot, and thicken it with
browned butter and flour; put it on to
come a-boil; then put in the balls and
all the other things, and let them boil
a while in the fauce; put in fome ketchup and cut pickles; never let the
pickles boil; lay the rump in the middle of a foup-difh, and the fauce about
it.　It is very good, although you keep
out the truffles, morels, pallets, and kernels. You need not put the forced meat
in the rump, except you pleafe; but
order it as in the beginning of the receipt.

To ſtew a Rump of Beef with Roots.

[*It is very good, and not very expenſive.*]

Seafon the beef in the fame way as in
the former receipt; brown it off in the
fame manner, and put it into a pot of
boiling

boiling water; let it ftew on a flow fire
with a good deal more water about it
than in the rich way of dreffing: it
makes a very good foup.   Take fome
carrot and turnip; parboil the carrots
with the beef: they give the foup a good
relifh : turn out the carrots and turnip
into a turner, or cut them in dices ;
brown a little butter, and thicken it with
flour ; lift up fome of the foup, and
fcum all the fat off it; thicken it with
browned butter and flour ; then put
the carrots and turnip into the fauce.
and let them boil until they are enough.
If you find the fauce not high enough
feafoned from the foup, put in more falt
and fpices and fome ketchup; throw an
onion or two into the pot, and ftrain
off the foup ; fcum the fat off it, and
put in toafted bread.   Difh the beef
with the fauce and roots around it.

Beef a-la-mode.

Take a rump of beef, and lard it with
bacon ; cut the pieces of bacon long ;
roll them in falt and mixed fpices before

fore you put them into the larding
pins; lay fome timber fkewers acrofs
the bottom of the pot; lay the beef on
them with two or three onions, a faggot of fweet herbs, and a gill of vinegar. You may cover the beef with the
fkin of the bacon. Put a wet cloth
round the mouth of the pot to keep in
the fteam; put the pot on a very flow
fire to ftew, till it is very tender; when
it has been two hours on the fire, turn
the beef in the pot, and clofe it up again
with the wet cloth. If it is a very large
piece, it will take five or fix hours in
doing; but whatever fize the beef is of,
it is enough when it is tender : take up
the meat, and ftrain off the foup; fcum
off all the fat very clean, and pour the
foup on the beef.

To pot Beef.

Take fome flices of a rump or a hook-
bone of beef; ftrew a little faltpetre on
it; let it lie two days; then put it in
the potting-can with a good deal of butter or fuet; tie it clofe up with paper,

and put it in a quick oven; let it bake
two or three hours; then take it out
and pour all the fat and gravy clean
from it. When it is cold, pull it all
into threads, and beat it very fine in a
mortar; feafon it with falt and mixed
fpices. Whatever weight of beef you
have, take the fame weight of fweet
butter; oil and fcum it; pour it on the
meat, and keep back the grounds. You
muft work the butter and meat very
well together; then prefs it into fmall
white pots, and oil fome more butter;
pour it on the top, and tie them clofe
up with paper. You may fend it in the
pots to the table. You may pot hare
in the fame manner.

To make minced Collops.

Take a tender piece of beef, keep out
all the fkin and fat, mince it fmall,
feafon it with falt and mixed fpices;
you may fhred an onion fmall, and put
in with it; fpread the collops, and
drudge flour on them; brown fome
butter in a frying-pan; put the collops
in

in the pan, and continue beating with
the beater till they fuck up all the butter, and be a little brown.   You may
draw as much ftock from the ſkins and
tough pieces as will ſerve for the ſauce;
ſtrain off the ſtock; ſet it on to boil,
and put the collops in, and let them
ſtew until they are enough.   You may
put in ſome pickles if you chooſe them.
If you ſee any of the butter on the top,
ſcum it.

To pot a Cow's Head.

Waſh it well with ſalt and water ; it
is the better of blanching a night, gi-
ving it more clean water; break it, that
it may go into the pot ; boil it until
the fleſh comes off eaſily ; take out the
eyes and the pallet: take the black ſkin
off the pallet ; cut the black out of the
eyes ; cut the eyes in rings, and the
pallet in dices, the fat parts about an
inch long, and mince the black parts
ſmall; then mix the pieces all together;
take the fat off the broth ; put the meat
into a pan, and all the fat, with a good
deal

deal of the broth; feafon it with falt
and mixed fpices; put it on, and let it
boil, ftirring it frequently; let it boil
until you find the meat tender, and
fuck up moft of the juice until it is like
a thick jelly about it, and then pot it
up. A calf's foot or two, cut in the
breadth of a ftraw, and about two inches long, mixed in the pan among the
reft fome time before it comes off, looks
very well.

To broil Beef Steaks.

Take the beft bit of the beef for
fteaks off the rib-end of a fparerib; cut
the fteaks pretty thick; brade them
with the flat fide of the chopen knife;
the gridiron muft be very clean and
very hot, the fire very clear, before you
lay them on; keep turning them often.
When enough falt them in the difh;
ftrew pickles over them. Send them hot
with a cover over them.

Scots (or ftewed) Beef Collops.

Cut your beef in fmall pieces; beat
them

them well; take a ftewpan, brown a little butter with flour, put in a row of
beef, with pepper, falt, and fliced onions; repeat the fame till your ftewpan
is near full; add two fpoonfuls of water to a middle-fized difh.   Cover the
the pan clofely on a clear fire; fhaking
the pan never take off the cover.   Ten
minutes will do them.

To make Beef Collops.

Cut thin flices of a tender piece of
beef pretty long, and about three inches
broad; cut the fat pieces feparate from
the lean; beat them with the rolling
pin; put a bit of fat on every piece of
lean; feafon them with falt and mixed
fpices; roll every one up like a collar;
pack them clofe to one another in a pot-
ting can; put butter above and below
them; then tie them clofe up with coarfe
paper; put them into the oven, and
bake them until they are enough.   If
you eat them hot, pour off all their
own juice, and fcum off all the fat;
thicken it with a little butter wrought
in

in flour, a little ketchup, and some cut
pickles in the sauce; pour it over the
collops; it makes a very pretty cold asset when you cut the roll in slices.

To collar Beef.

Take the nineholes of beef; bone it;
rub it well with salt and saltpetre; let
it lie three or four days, or more, according to the thickness of the beef;
take it up and dry it well with a cloth;
then season it very well with mixed spices and sweet herbs, if you choose it;
roll it up very hard, and roll a cloth a-
bout it; tie the cloth very tight at both
ends : bind the whole collar very firm
with broad tape; put it into a pot of
boiling water; be sure to keep it always
covered with water. If it is very thick,
it will take near four hours boiling.
When it is boiled hang it up by one
of the ends of the cloth, to drop the water from it ; when it is cold, loose it out
of the bindings. You may make a collar of pork the very same way ; it takes
always a little more boiling than beef.

Scarlet

Scarlet Beef.

Take a piece of a breaſt of very fat
beef; blanch it twenty-four hours in
cold water : then drop the water very
well from it, and dry it very well with
a cloth ; rub it well with brown ſugar, ſalt, and ſaltpetre ; turn it every
day for a fortnight, and then boil it.
It eats very well hot with greens, and
when ſliced down, makes a very pretty
cold aſſet.

To ſtew a Fillet of Veal.

Cut off the ſhank-bone, and make
holes in the veal; after ſtuffing it with
forc'd meat, rub it over with an egg,
and duſt it with flour, then brown it.
When the veal boils, put in as much
ſtock as will cover it ; cover the pot
very cloſe, and let it ſtew on a ſlow fire ;
turn it often as the liquor waſtes. When
it is enough, take up ſome of the liquor ; ſcum off the fat, and thicken it
with a little butter wrought in flour ;
put in ſome pickled oyſters, and a little

tle of their liquor, a large glafs of white wine, and the fqueeze of a lemon. You may boil a piece of lemon-peel and a blade of mace in it ; but be fure to take them out before difhing; give it a fcrape of nutmeg ; then difh the veal, and pour the fauce over it. The fhank, or any piece of frefh meat, will make a very good ftock for it.

To make Scotch Collops.

Cut thin flices out of the thick of the thigh ; beat them with a rolling pin, and brown them with frefh butter; boil with the ftock a piece of lemon-peel, fome mace, and a glafs of wine; ftrain it off, and thicken it with a little butter wrought in flour ; put in fome pickled oyfters ; then put in the collops, and don't let them get above three or four boils; beat the yolk of an egg, and mix in two or three fpoonfuls of fweet cream and a fcrape of nutmeg; mix it with the collops, and give them two or three tof-fes above the fire; but do not let them boil ; falt them properly.

Garnifh all veal-difhes with fliced lemon ;

mon; you may put in forc'd-meat balls
if you pleafe.

To hafh Cold Veal.

Cut it down in thin flices : take the
bones and fkinny pieces to make the
ftock of; boil a piece of lemon-peel and
a blade of mace. If there has been any
of the gravy left of the roaft, put it into
the ftock ; then ftrain off the flock, and
thicken it with butter and flour as a-
bove ; put in a little ketchup and the
fqueeze of a lemon, if you pleafe ; it is
much better of a little wine ; then put
in the veal, and give it a boil or two,
and then difh it on fippets of toafted
bread.

To mince Cold Veal.

Cut off all the brown'd pieces and
fat ; mince the white part of the meat
fmall with a knife ; boil fome fweat
cream (taking care to ftir it until it
boils, to keep it from bratting); thick-
en it with a very little fweat butter
knead in flour ; put in the veal, and feafon

fon it with the grate of lemon, a little falt, and the fcrape of a nutmeg; keep it toffing on the fire until the fauce is a little thick; juft before it comes off, give it a little fqueeze of a lemon: fo ferve it up.

To make Veal Cutlets.

After cutting the back ribs of veal into fteaks, brod them with the choppin-knife; flour them before you put them into the frying-pan; make them of a fine light brown; make a ragoo fauce of fome ftock; thicken it with brown'd butter and flour, as in the other receipts for brown fauce, and the fame kind of feafoning; then put in the fteaks into the fauce; let them ftew until they are enough: fo ferve them up.

Broil'd Veal Cutlets.

Cut and beat them as in the former receipt; rub them all over with a beat egg; feafon them with falt and the grate of a lemon; ftrew fome crumbs of bread over them on both fides; pour

a

a little oiled fweet butter over them ;
lay every cutlet in clean white paper ;
broil them on a clear fire, turning them
often until they are enough ; take off
the paper, and difh them : for fauce,
fend up fome beat butter, ketchup, and
the fqueeze of a lemon, in a fauce-boat.

To fricafee a Breaft of Veal.

Cut down the ribs of the breaft ;
break them into fhort pieces, and wafh
them very clean ; let them lie fome time
in water to blanch. You may put in a
little milk or flour, to help to whiten
the meat; then put it into a clofe goblet
with boiling water ; put in a tied bunch
of parfley, a blade of mace, and fome
lemon peel with it; let the meat boil
tender ; caft fome yolks of eggs, and
mix a little cream, white wine, fome falt,
the fcrape of a nutmeg, and the fqueeze
of a lemon with them ; thicken fome
of the broth the meat is boiled in with
a very little fweet butter knead in flour;
and when it boils, ftir it in gradually
among the eggs ; take the meat quite
away

away from the broth, and put it into
the fauce-pan; pour the fauce on it until it thicken; but be fure never to let
any thing come a-boil that eggs are in,
elfe it will curdle the fauce.

You may fricafee any white meat in
the fame way; fuch as lamb, chickens,
rabbits, tripe, pallets, and kernels, &c.

To make Veal Fricandos.

Cut the back-ribs, keeping two of
them together; make a ftock of the
fhank, neck, and any coarfe pieces;
make up a faggot of fweet herbs, winter
favory, thyme, and parfley; put it into
the ftock, with a few onions, fome lemon-peel, whole pepper, a little white
wine, the fqueeze of a lemon, a few
cloves, and a blade of mace. If you
choofe, you may put in an anchovy.
When the ftock is enough, ftrain it off,
and thicken it with butter knead in flour;
when it comes a-boil, put in the ftakes,
and ftew them on a flow fire. When
you difh it, put in any kind of pickles
                                    or

or not as you pleafe; be fure to brown
the ribs in the frying-pan before you
put them into the fauce.

To make Veal Olives.

Take ten or twelve veal collops, cut
them thin, and a good deal longer than
broad; rub them all over with an egg;
then cover them all over with forc'd
meat; roll them up, and pack them
clofe to one another, in any thing that
will hold them, and fire them in the
oven; when they are enough, lay them
neatly in the difh, putting a ragoo of
pallets and kernels over them.

To drefs a Calf's Head.

After fcalding and wafhing it very
clean, lay it in cold water to blanch;
boil it, but not too much; when it is
cold, cleave it quite exactly through the
middle; take one half of the head; take
out the tongue and pallet; cut off the
upftanding part of the ear; ftrike off
the end of the nofe; fcore it in fquares;
rub it over with a beat egg; then ftrew
it

it over with falt, mixed fpices, and crumbs of bread ; lay pieces of butter upon it, and put it before the fire to brown, bafting it frequently with the butter. Remember, when cleaning the head, not to open the jaws. Cut down the other half into flices, neither too long nor too fhort ; flice off the ear-part round ways, and take out the eye ; cut the black out of it, and flice it down ; fkin the tongue and pallet, and flice them down ; thicken fome ftock of beef with butter knead in flour ; feafon it with falt, mixed fpices, a little ketchup, fome white wine, the fqueeze of a le- mon, and fome pickled oyfters ; put in the hafh, and let it ftew a little ; throw in a piece of lemon-peel, but take it out when you difh it. If you want it done in the higheft way, it fhould have forc'd meat balls, truffles, morels, and pickled mufhrooms ; but it is a good difh without thefe four ar- ticles. When you difh it, lay the hafh in the difh, and the other half in the middle ;

middle; garnifh with the brain, cakes, and fliced lemon.

To make Brain Cakes.

When the head is cloven, take out the brains; take out any ftrings that may be amongft them, and caft them well with a knife; then put in a little raw egg, a fcrape of nutmeg, and a little falt, and mix them with flour to make them ftick together; caft them fmooth; then drop them like bifcuits into a pan of boiling butter, and fry them on both fides a fine brown.

Lambs brains are done in the fame manner.

To Turtle a Calf's Head.

Put the head in a pot to boil for half an hour; cut it into fmall pieces; you muft have a very ftrong ftock of beef; make a faggot of parfley, onions, and fweet herbs; it muft be very high feafoned with fpices; put in a little Cayenne pepper; ftrain the ftock from the herbs, and put the minced meat into the ftock,

with

with a mutchkin (pint) of Madeira, the
yolks of four hard eggs chopt, and a
good piece of the lean of bacon-ham;
let all boil together until the head is
tender, and the gravy well-foked in;
then take out the ham; have a fricafee-
fauce ready to pour on it; give it a tofs
on the fire to mix it: the garnifhing is
a pafte round the difh.

To pot a Calf's Head.

Boil it about half an hour; flice as
many round pieces off the ear as you
can; cut out the black of the eyes, and
flice them into rings; cut the fkinny
pieces about an inch long, and fome a
little longer; fome about the breadth
of a ftraw, and fome of them broader;
cut the flefhy parts of the head pretty
fmall; have fome beef-ftock; boil a
blade of mace, a little lemon-peel, and a
fprig of winter favory in it; ftrain it
off; clarify it with the white of eggs,
and run it through a jelly-bag; cut the
pallet into fmall fquares; put all the
meat in the ftock, and feafon it with a
little

little white pepper and falt; let it boil
until the ftock is well-foked in; put a
little of the thinneft of it into the bottom of a ftone bowl, and let it cool;
take fome pickled bitroot and pickled
cucumber; cut them in fuch fhapes as
that you can lay them in the form of a
flower on the jelly, that is, in the bottom of the bowl; lay a tire of the ftew-
meat over it: as you lift the meat, pick
out the rounds of the ears and eyes, and
lay them afide on a plate; lay on fome
more of the meat, until there is about
the half of it in; then take the rounds
of the ears and the eyes that you kept
out, and flip them down edge-ways as
near to the fide of the bowl as you can;
let there be a little diftance between
every round; put in the reft of the meat
round the edge of the bowl; put fliced
bitroot and kidney-beans, or any thing
that is green at the time, about with the
bitroot, or any thing that is fhowy; it
muft be thoroughly cold before it is
turned out of the bowl. If it does not
come eafily out, put the bowl into warm
water,

water, but let it ftand very fhort time in the water; then turn it out on your difh.

To make Mutton Cutlets.

Cut the back-ribs or loin of mutton into ftakes, and beat them with the chopping-knife; brown them in a frying-pan; then ftrew crumbs of bread over them; feafon them with falt and fpices; have as much good ftock as will cover the ftakes; put a little ketchup in the fauce; it is much better of a little red wine; when the fauce comes a-boil, put the ftakes into a clofe pan; let them ftew until they are enough. In cafe the fauce be not thick enough with the bread, put in a little butter wrought in flour; ftrew fome cut pickles on the ftakes when you difh them.

To hafh Cold Cutlets.

Cut the mutton down in thin flices; break the bones, and take any pieces of the mutton that does not go into the hafh; it makes the ftock the better.
You

You may boil an onion or two in it.
When the ftock is ready, thicken it
with brown'd butter and flour; put in
a little ketchup and fome falt and fpices;
when the fauce is boiled, throw in the
hafh, and let it get two or three quick
boils. If there was any of the cold gravy left, put it into the fauce, taking care
not to put in any of the fat along with
it. All hafhes are much the better of
cut pickles in them., Difh it on fippits
of toafted bread. Cold roaft beef or
lamb may be hafhed in the fame manner.

To make a Haricot of Mutton.

After cutting off the flap of a loin of
mutton, cut the reft into ftakes, and
beat them with the chopping-knife;
brown them in a frying-pan; lay them
on a dilh, and feafon them with falt and
fpices on both fides; have fome carrots
and turnips turned; if you have not a
turner, cut them into fquares; be fure
that the carrots are parboiled before you
cut them; have as much ftock as will

cover

cover the meat and roots; thicken it
with brown'd butter and flour; then
put in the ſtakes, carrot, and turnip,
and all the gravy that runs from the
ſtakes, into a cloſe pan, and let them
ſtew until they are enough; lay the
ſtakes in a ſoup-diſh, and the roots
and ſauce over them.

*To dreſs a Diſh of Mutton with Paper
in place of Coals, which is thought to
eat ſweeter than when done on the common Fire.*

Cut down the back-ribs in ſtakes, and
flat them with a chopping-knife; pare
ſome turnip, and ſlice them very thin;
ſlice alſo ſome bread and an onion or
two very thin; mix the turnip, bread,
and onion together; ſeaſon the ſtakes
with a little ſalt and ſpices; lay a row
of the ſtakes in the bottom of a necromancer*, then a row of the bread
and roots, and ſo continue until it is
full; tie the necromancer by the handles
be-

* A necromancer is a flat white-iron pan, with two
handles, and a lid that checks in very cloſe.

between two chairs; have a tea-kettle of boiling water; fill up the pan with it, and put on the lid very clofe; have ready fome wafte-paper ftripped through your hand; light one piece after another, and hold it below the bottom of the pan, moving the lighted paper backwards and forwards, and it will be ready in lefs than a quarter of an hour. Send it to the table in the necromancer, with a plate below it.

To boil a Leg of Lamb with Cabbage or Cauliflower.

Cut off the loin and boil the gigot; cut the loin into ftakes, and fry them of a fine brown; put the boiled lamb in the middle of the difh; put a fried ftake, and a little young cabbage or cauliflower for each ftake, round the boiled lamb; pour fome beat butter over it; take care not to boil the lamb too much.

Lamb covered with Rice.

Half roaft a fore-leg of lamb; cut it
in

in pieces as for a pie ; feafon it with falt, and lay it in a difh, according to the fize of the lamb. If the lamb is not very fat, put in a piece of butter in the bottom of the difh and a little water. If the difh be any thing large, it will take a pound of rice ; wafh the rice very clean, and put it on with as much water as will boil it foft, and don't take it off the fire until all the water is fuck'd up ; put in fome blades of mace with it. When the rice is thus prepared, ftir in a good piece of frefh butter, a little falt, and the fcrape of a nutmeg, amongft the warm rice; caft four eggs, and mix them up with the rice, keeping out a little of the eggs; then lay all the rice over the difh ; rub the top of the difh with the egg you kept out ; put it in the oven, and let it bake until the rice is firm, and of a fine light brown.

To drefs a Lamb's Head.

Wafh it very clean ; let it blanch as long as you can in cold water ; parboil it ; cut off the neck, and cleave the head

juft

juft as you do a calf's head ; take out
the brains ; rub the head over with an
egg ; have fome parfley and chieves, or
young onions, finely fhred, mixed with
crumbs of bread ; ftrew it all over the
head, and put it down before the fire to
crifp, bafting it well with butter ; take
out the tongue when you cleave the
head ; mince all the flefh you can get
off the neck very fmall, with the tongue
and pluck ; take up fome of the water
that boiled the head and pluck ; put in
the bones of the neck, and about half
of the liver, and boil them until all the
ftrength is out of them ; put in a piece
of lemon-peel, if you have it.   When
the ftock is enough ftrain it off ; thicken
it with a little butter kned in flour ; put
the minced meat into the fauce, with
fhred parfley and chieves, a little ketchup, a proper quantity of falt and fpices, and the fqueeze of a lemon. If you
choofe it, order the brains as in the receipt for the brain-cakes ; cut the other
half of the liver into ftripes, and fry it ;
put the hafh in the difh, and the head

in

in the middle of it, and garnifh with
the liver and brains.

To drefs Chickens with Peafe and Lettuce.

Take as many good peafe and chickens
as will fill the difh you intend; trufs the
chickens as for boiling; feafon them
with fpices and falt; put a piece of frefh
butter in every one of them ; tie up a
faggot of parfley, a fprig of young onions, and a fprig of thyme or winter favory ; put the peafe in the pan, with a
piece of frefh butter; ftrew in a little
falt and fpices ; put in the faggot of
fweet herbs; lay the chickens above the
peafe, with the breafts undermoft; fplit
the hearts of two or three lettuces, and
wafh them very clean; put them above
the chickens with about half a mutchkin of water, to keep the peafe from
burning; clofe up the goblet, and put
it on a flow fire to ftove ; it does not
take long time to do ; lay the chickens
with their breafts uppermoft in a foup-
difh, with the peafe and lettuce over
them, and as much of the broth as the
                                        difh

diſh will hold; take out the faggot of
ſweet herbs; ſo ſerve them up.

To make Veal or Lamb Toaſts.

Take the kidney, with all the fat be-
longing to it, and a little piece lean out
of the thick of the thigh ; mince it ſo
fine that it will ſpread on your fingers;
ſeaſon it with ſalt, grate of lemon, and
nutmeg. You may take ſome ſmall
ſhred parſley, if you chooſe; mix all
together, and work it up with a raw
egg; cut ſome ſlices not too thin; cut
the bread into any ſhape you pleaſe either long or round; cover them with
the minced meat pretty thick, and raiſe
it a little higher in the middle; put them
in a pan of boiling butter, with the
bread ſide undermoſt. You muſt fry
it gradually, elſe the bread will burn
and the meat will be cold in the heart;
turn it to the other ſide, and fry it a
fine brown.

A Jugged Hare.

Cut the hare in pieces; put a pretty
large

large piece of butter in the bottom of a
long jug; feafon it with falt and mixed
fpices; then pack in as many of the beft
pieces of the hare as the jug will hold ;
put in a faggot of fweet herbs, and two
or three onions amongft them ; take
fome of the water you wafhed the hare
in, and ftrain it through a fearce ; fill up
the jug with it, and tie the mouth of it
very clofe with feveral folds of paper ;
put it into a pot of cold water ; the water muft not come up farther than the
neck of the jug, elfe it will boil into it;
as the water boils in, you muft put in
more to keep it of an equal quantity.
If it is an old hare, it will take three
hours of doing ; the butter will rife to
the top; pour it clean off; take out the
herbs and onions when you difh it, and
pour the fauce over it; be fure to tie
the jug to the handles of the pot.

A Good Scotch Haggies.

Make the haggies-bag perfectly clean;
parboil the draught; boil the liver very
well, fo as it will grate; dry the meal
before

before the fire; mince the draught and
a pretty large piece of beef very small;
grate about half of the liver; mince
plenty of the suet and some onions small;
mix all these materials very well together, with a handful or two of the dried
meal: spread them on the table, and
season them properly with salt and mixed spices; take any of the scrapes of beef
that is left from mincing, and some of
the water that boiled the draught, and
make about a choppen of good stock of
it; then put all the haggies-meat into
the bag, and that broath in it: then sew
up the bag; but be sure to put out all
the wind before you sew it quite close.
If you think the bag is thin, you may
put it in a cloth. If it is a large haggies, it will take at least two hours
boiling.

A Lamb's Haggies.

Clean the bag very well; slit up all
the little fat tripes and the rodikin with
a pair of scissars, and wash them very
clean; parboil them, and what kernels
you

you can get about the lamb ; then cut them in little pieces, but not too fmall ; fhred the web very fmall, and mix it with the other cut meat, and feafon it properly with a little falt and fpices; caft three eggs with three fpoonfuls of flour, as for pancake-batter ; mix them up with a mutchkin of fweet milk; have a handful of young parfley, and fome chieves or young onions, fhred very fmall ; then mix all the materials very well into the batter ; put all into the bag, and few it up : it will take about an hour's boiling.

A Pudding of Lamb's Blood.

Take as much blood as with half a mutchkin of cream will fill an affet ; mix the blood and cream together, and run it through a fearce ; feafon it with falt and fpices, a fprig of mint and chieves, or young onions, minced fmall ; mince the fat of the near or kidneys fmall ; mix all together, and fire it in the oven, or in a frying-pan. Lamb's blood is the fweeteft of all blood.

To

To make Puddings either of Sheep or Cow's Blood.

Break all the clots of the blood very well; run it through a fearce; mix fome new milk with it, according to the quantity of blood; feafon it properly with falt and pepper; fhred fome onions and a little mint; cut the fuet, but in very fmall pieces; do not be fparing of the fuet; mix in a little oat-meal; fill the ftuff into the fkins; cut them all of one fize, and tie the two ends together; be fure that the water is boiling, either to haggies or puddings. Juft when you are going to put them in, pour in a little cold water to put it off the boil, elfe they will be ready to burft. When they are in a while, prick them with a pin to let out the wind.

To make Liver Puddings.

Boil the liver very well, and grate it down; take an equal quantity of grated bread and liver; cut fome onions and plenty of fuet; feafon properly with

falt

falt and fpices, and fill them in the white end of the pudding.

To make Apple Puddings.

Cut the apples pretty fmall; have fome bread grated, clean'd currants and fugar; mix them all together; feafon them with cinnamon and nutmeg; moiften them with a little white wine; cut the fuet, and mix all together; put them in the fkins, and cut them all of an equal length, not too long, and tie them at both ends.

To make Rice Puddings.

Wafh the rice very clean through two or three waters; put it on in a pan with a little milk to burft; keep it ftirring while it is on the fire, for fear of burning; when it has fucked up all the milk, take it off, and let it cool; mix it with fome currants; feafon it properly with nutmeg, cinnamon, and fugar. You may put in fome grate of lemon, if you have it; mix the fuet with the reft of the meat, and fill them into the fkins;

be

be sure not to cut the suet too small for any puddings in the skin, for it boils away, and makes the puddings eat dry.

To make Almond Puddings in Skins.

Beat half a pound of sweet almonds with brandy, half a pound of sugar-biscuit, and a pound of beef suet ; mix all together, and season it with cinnamon, nutmeg, and sugar, and some grate of lemon, if you have it; then fill up the skins.

To roast a Calf's or Lamb's Liver.

Lard it, and fasten it on the spit; baste it with butter. The best sauce for a roasted liver is beat butter with ketchup, and a little vinegar mixed with it.

To ragoo a Liver.

Cut it in thin slices; brown some butter, and fry the liver in it; take the liver out from the butter, and dust a little flour amongst the butter, and pour in some boiling water; have some parsley

fley and young onions fmall fhred ; let
them boil a little in the fauce ; feafon it
with ketchup, a little vinegar, and falt ;
put in the liver and let it get two or
three boils ; garnifh it with fried parfley.   You may do cow's nears or kidneys in the fame manner.

To make Cake-jelly of Calves Feet.

Take nine or a dozen gang of calves
feet ; fcald them very well ; flit them
up, and lay them amongft lukewarm
water for feveral hours ; put them on in
a large pot.   When they are fo well
boiled that the bones will come out,
take all the bones from them ; put all
the meat back into the pot, and let it
boil until the whole fubftance is out of
it ; ftrain it through a hair fearce into
an earthen veffel that will hold it ; while
it is warm, fcum all the fat you can off
it ; let it ftand all night ; and if there is
any fat remaining on it, take it clean off,
when you take it out of the veffel, cut
all the fediment from the bottom of it ;
then put the ftock into a clean brafs pan ;

fet

fet it on a fire neither too ftrong nor too flow ; it muft boil until it is very thick and appears almoft black in the pan ; then turn it out as thin as you can on ftone plates; when it is cool, take it from the plates, and lay it at a diftance from the fire to dry gradually ; when it is quite dry, and looks clear and hard like horn, you may lay it by ; and when you intend to ufe it in jelly, to one ounce of it put a mutchkin and a gill of cold water, and put it on the fire ; when it is diffolved, it is ready to make jelly of. You order it in the fame way as if you were making jelly of frefh calves feet. This is a moft ufeful thing in a family, if it is wanted for the table or a fick perfon in a hurry ; it is very good, and looks pretty. You may put in a little heartfhorn alongft with it.

To make Portable Soup.

Take a very large hough of beef, a large knuckle of veal, and a good old cock; take off all the fkin and fat from them ; cut them clean from the bones;

put

put them on with five or fix pints of water ; let it boil on a flow fire till it become a very ftrong jelly, which you will know by taking out a little of it to cool; when very ftrong, run it through a hair fearce, and let it fettle. If there is any fat on the top, be fure to fcum it off; then put it into ftone tea-cups ; take care that you let none of the fedi-ment into the cups ; fet them into a pan of cold water ; put them on a flow fire, and let the water boil gently, until the jelly is as thick as glue ; take care the water does not boil into the jelly ; when you fee it come to the thicknefs of jelly, take out the cups and let them cool ; then turn out the glue on a piece of clean flannel ; keep it turning every fix or feven hours on a dry place of the flannel till they are quite dry ; put every one of them into white paper, and hang them up in a dry place; when you intend to ufe it, pour as much boiling water on the glue as will fill the difh you want ; keep it ftirring all the time until it diffolves. You may make

it

it of what degree of ftrength you pleafe, by putting in lefs or more of the glue. You may feafon it properly with mixed fpices and falt; let it fettle a little before you pour it into the diſh; the fpices will fall to the bottom. If you have this, you can never be at a lofs for a fauce, by diffolving a piece of it.

To ragoo Pallets and Kernels.

Boil the pallets until the ſkin come off them that they are very tender; par-boil the kernels until you can get the fleſhy pieces to come off them; fry them a light brown; make the ſtock of the fleſh that comes off the kernels; put in a blade of mace, about half a dozen of cloves, and fome whole pepper, and a piece of lemon-peel; when the ſtock is ſtrong enough, ſtrain it off; thicken it with a little butter wrought in flour, and a little white wine in it; cut the pallets in fquares, and put them and the kernels into the fauce, and let them ſtew until they are enough; when you are about to diſh them, put in them a
few

few cut pickles, and garnifh the difh with fliced lemon ; falt them properly.

Hare Collops.

Hare collops are dreffed in the fame manner as beef minced collops; only add a little claret in the fauce.

To roaſt a Hare.

Work fome crumbs of bread and currants with a good deal of frefh butter, and feafon it with fugar, falt, and nutmeg; work them up with a beat egg; then put it into the hare, and few up the belly ; draw up the thighs to the body, to make it as fhort as poffible ; fkewer the head even, or as it were looking over its fhoulder; fpit it, and lay it to a clear fire, having firft bafted it with butter; beat the yolk of an egg, and mix it with cream. When the butter is well dropped from it, pour it clean out of the pan ; then keep it clofe bafting with the cream until it is almoft taken up. When the hare is ready, have fome more cream warm ; then take all that is dropped from the hare

and

and mix it with the cream; diſh the hare, pour on the cream-ſauce over it. ——Or take the following ſauce: Take half claret and half water; cut ſome very thin ſlices of bread, and a little piece of freſh butter; let it all boil till it is pretty ſmooth; ſweeten it properly, and put in a ſcrape of nutmeg.

To ſmother Rabbits.

Truſs them as you do a roaſted hare; put them into as much boiling water as will cover them; peel a good many onions, and boil them in water whole; take ſome of the liquor the rabbits are boiled in, and put in a good piece of butter knead in flour; then put in the onions amongſt it, keeping them breaking until the ſauce be pretty thick; diſh the rabbits, and pour the ſauce over them all except the heads. The ſame ſauce ſerves for a boiled gooſe and boiled ducks.

To make a Caparata.

Cut down a cold fowl, and take all the ſkin and fat of it except the rump; mince

mince all the meat very fmall with a
knife; break the bones of it, and put
them on with fome water, lemon-peel,
and a blade of mace; let them boil until all the fubftance is out of them;
ftrain it off, and thicken it with a little
butter knead in flour; chop fome yolks
of hard eggs; put the minced fowl and
eggs into the fauce; let it get two or
three boils; juft before difhing, put in
the fqueeze of a lemon, a fcrape of nutmeg, and a proper quantity of falt;
broil the back of the fowl, and lay it
on the top of the caparata. A cold
roafted turkey may be done in the fame
manner.

General Rules for boiling Fowls.

A young middling turkey will take
three quarters of an hour; if it is large,
you muft give allowance accordingly;
a hen will take half an hour, and a
chicken a quarter of an hour. They
are the better of being blanched a while
in

in milk and water, and are much better
of having their breafts rubbed with a
piece of butter; boil them in a clean
cloth. All boiled meat, whether poultry
or butcher-meat, fhould have plenty
of water, and be boiled on a quick fire;
for there is a great difference betwixt
boiling and ftewing any thing. The
proper fauces for all boiled poultry is a
parfley, oyfter, fellery, or cream fauce.

A Parfley Sauce.

Pick and wafh the parfley very well;
put it into boiling water, and boil it
tender; drain the water from it; chop
it very fmall, and mix beat butter a-
mongft it.

An Oyfter Sauce.

Clean the oyfters well, and fcald them;
then boil them up in beat butter, and a
little of their own liquor.

A Sellery Sauce.

Cut the white ends of the fellery in
pieces of about an inch long; boil it in
water

water till it is tender ; thicken a little ftock with butter knead in flour ; put in the fellery and a blade of mace, and let it boil a little.

A Cream Sauce.

Take fome fweet cream ; let it come a-boil, ftirring it clofe to keep it from bratting ; caft the yolks of three or four eggs, and mix in a little cold cream along with them ; then mix the boiling cream gradually amongft the eggs ; turn it backwards and forwards to make it fmooth ; put it on the fire to warm, but do not let it boil ; ftir it all the time : fweeten it a little with fugar, and give it a fcrape of nutmeg. Some choofe it without fugar ; in that cafe, put in a little falt.

To boil Beef or Mutton in the juice.

To every pound of beef allow a quarter of an hour ; two hours will boil a large gigot of mutton. You muft take care, when taking it out of the pot, not to run a fork into it, elfe the whole

juice

juice will run from it. You may put carrots and turnip, or cauliflower, about it, and pour a little beat butter over the mutton. In place of roots, you may give it a caper fauce, if you choofe it.

To roaſt any piece of Veniſon.

Lard it, and feafon it with mixed fpices and falt; let it lie four or five hours in fome claret or lemon-juice, turning it every hour; then fpit and roaſt it at a gentle fire; baſte it with the wine that it lay in; take that which drops from it, and add fome gravy to it; thicken it with butter knead in flour, and a little ketchup; boil it up, and pour it on the venifon.

To ſtew Veniſon.

Cut it in thin flices, and put it into a ſtew-pan with fome claret, fugar, a little vinegar, and fried crumbs of bread; feafon it properly with falt and fpices; let it ſtew until it is enough.

Veni-

Venifon in the Blood.

Bone a fhoulder or a breaft of venifon ; let it lie in its own blood for a night ; take it up, and feafon it with falt and fpices : take fome winter fāvory, fweet marjoram, and thyme ; fhred them very fmall with fome beef-fuet chopped fmall ; put it in a pan with the herbs, and ftir it on the fire until it is thick ; then fpread it all over the venifon with fome of the blood ; roll it up in a collar, and bind it. You may, if you choofe, roaft it on the fpit, or ftove it in gravy with fome claret and fhallots. Serve it up hot. Send up to the table with all roafted venifon a faucer of currant jelly.

To ftew Venifon that has been oafted.

Take fome gravy, claret, a bunch of fweet herbs, and a little ketchup; brown fome butter ; thicken it with flour, and put it into the fauce with falt and fpices ; let all boil until it is fmooth ; cut the venifon in thin flices, put it into the
fauce,

sauce, and give it one boil; take out the herbs, give it the squeeze of a lemon, and then dish it.

To boil Venison.

Cut the venison into slices of about half an inch thick; season them with salt and spices and crumbs of bread; broil them on a clear fire, and give them a gravy sauce.

To broil a Haunch of Venison.

Salt it for a week; put it into boiling water; if it is large it will take two hours and a half to boil. You may send it up with cauliflower, or any kind of garden-stuff you choose, with melted butter.

Venison makes the finest of minced collops. You order them in the same way as you do the beef or hare collops.

To roast and stuff a Turkey.

Slit it up at the back of the neck; take out the crop; make the stuffing

of

of crumbs of bread and currants, a little fugar, and a fcrape of nutmeg; work it up with a piece of frefh butter and a beat egg; fill up the breaft with it, and fkewer it with the head looking over the wing; it muft be well floured and bafted with butter, and roafted with a clear quick fire; put a gravy-fauce under it; make a fauce of fome thin fliced bread, fome water, a little white wine, a blade of mace, fome fugar, and a piece of frefh butter; let all boil until it is very fmooth, and do not let it be too thick. Send it up in a fauce-boat.

The beft Sauce for a roafted Hen.

Take a gravy or an egg fauce. When you roaft fmall chickens, they look the better to be ftuffed with crumbs of bread, fmall fhred parfley, and a little falt wrought up with a good piece of frefh butter; fill up the bellies with it. Young chickens require a little beat butter poured over them.

To

To roast a Goose or Duck.

A goose or duck is the better of being rubbed with pepper and salt within: some choose a sprig of sage in them. A goose is the better of being rubbed with salt on its outside two or three days before it is roasted. You salt the ducks on the spit. Dish up the goose with gravy sauce, and garnish it with raw onions; send up a plateful of apple-sauce along with it: When you draw the ducks off the spit, pour a glass of red wine through them, and mix them well with the gravy. Green geese and young ducklings, the newer they are killed the better before you put them to the fire; dish them with gravy-sauce; serve up some gooseberry-sauce made thus: Put some green gooseberries on with some water, a piece of fresh butter and sugar. Some choose this sauce to roasted chickens.

To dress a Wild Duck.

Half roast it, and score it on the breast;

breaft ; put pepper and falt, and the juice of a lemon, on every fcore ; lay the breaft undermoft in a ftew-pan with a little gravy; let it ftew a little ; then difh it, and put a glafs of claret in the gravy, and two or three fhallots fhred fmall ; pour it over the ducks.

To ragoo a pair of Ducks.

Draw them ; and take the gizzards and the necks, and put them on to boil for a ftock for the fauce ; finge the ducks, and feafon them within with falt and fpices ; duft them with flour, and brown them on all fides in a frying-pan; then take them out, and ftrew fome falt and fpices on them ; ftrain off the ftock, and thicken it with browned butter and flour ; put in fome red wine, ketchup, and walnut pickle, or the fqueeze of a lemon ; put the ducks into the fauce with fome whole onions ; clofe up the pan, and let them ftew until they are tender; fcum all the fat of the fauce, and pour it on the ducks, and the whole onions with it.

To

To make a Tame Duck pafs for a Wild one.

Knock it on the head with a ftick, that the blood may go through the body of it; drefs it in the fame way you do the wild ducks, and you will not know the difference.

To pot Geefe the French way.

Put in what number of geefe you choofe to pot ; feed them on corn and water; clean out their place every day, and give them clean ftraw to lie on ; they muft be fed very fat, or they are not worth doing. Cut off the legs and wings, with as much of the breaft to them as you can; rub the legs and wings very well with faltpetre, and lay them thirty-fix hours in it, but no long-er; take all the feam, and ftrip all the fat off the guts ; put the fat into a pot to boil, and when it is all melted, put in the legs and wings, and let them boil in the greafe until they are enough ; then take them up, and put them into a ftone jar, and pour in all the fat on them ;
when

when they are cold, have fome mutton-
fuet rhinded, and fill up the jar, and tie
up the pot with leather; they keep a
long time.   If you eat them cold, wafh
off the fat with a little warm water,
but they eat much better when hot ;
they are warmed thus : Put a leg and a
wing in a pan, with as much of the fat
as will cover them, and let them boil in
it until they are warm at the heart.   Let
none of the fat go to the table.

A general Rule for roaſting Wild Fowl.

To all wild fowl the fpit fhould be
very hot before you put them on it ;
fkewer them with their legs acrofs ; cut
off only the feet ; and for the rough-
footed wild fowl, fuch as black-cock and
muir-fowl, you keep all their feet on
them, clofe bafting with butter ; difh
them on toafted bread, and pour plenty
of beat frefh butter over them.   When
you roaſt wood-cock or ſnipe, do not cut
the heads off them nor gut them; fkewer
them with their own bill ; bafte them
well with butter ; put toafted bread below

low them, to keep what drops from the gut; dish them on the toast, and pour beat butter over them.

To pot any kind of Wild Fowl.

Draw the fowls, and truss them; season them with salt and mixed spices, and pack them in the potting-can with a good deal of fresh butter; close up the pot, and bake them in the oven; when enough, pour off the butter and gravy from them; scum all the butter off the gravy, and add more to it. You may put them in small pots, and cover them with the melted butter. You may pot partridges or muir-fowl in the same way as you do hare and beef; but remember the partridges, muir-fowl, and hare, must be either baked or roasted before you thread them, and order them as you do the beef. Venison is potted in the same manner.

To pot Pigeons.

Draw and truss them; season them well within with mixed spices and salt; put

put a piece of butter within every one of them ; put them in the potting-can with their breasts undermoft, and some butter about them, and throw some of the mixed fpices and falt over them ; put in a little water with them, and clofe them up. You may do them either in the oven or in a pot on the fire ; but they are much the beft in an oven.

To ftove Pigeons.

Stuff them with forced meat; have some good broth ready, and when it boils, put in the pigeons; take the hearts of fome cabbage-lettuce, and quarter them, put them in with the pigeons, and two or three green onions ; feafon them with mixed fpices and falt, and thicken it with butter knead in flour ; clofe them up in the goblet, and let them ftew till they are ready ; then lay the pigeons in the middle of the difh with the lettuce over them, and pour fome of their own broth into the difh.

To

To ragoo Pigeons.

Trufs the pigeons as for boiling, and
feafon them within with fpices and falt;
brown fome butter in a frying-pan;
duft the pigeons with flour; put them
in the frying-pan, and make them of a
fine brown; turn them often in the pan
until they are alike browned; take them
out, and lay them on a difh. You may
make a very rich ftock of the gizzards,
pinions, livers, and hearts; wafh them
very clean, and put them on with fome
water, an onion, a faggot of parfley,
and winter favory; let all boil until the
ftrength is out of them; ftrain it off,
and turn it into a clean pan, keeping
back the grounds; thicken it with
browned butter and flour, and put in
fome red wine; feafon it with falt and
fpices, a little ketchup, and truffles and
morels, if you choofe: Put the pigeons
in a ftew-pan, and let them ftew on a
flow fire; difh them neatly with their
fhoulders outmoft, putting one in the
middle; cut fome pickles, and mix them
in

in the fauce, and pour it on them. If it is the feafon for afparagus, it looks very pretty to put a few between every pigeon, with the tops outmoft.

To broil Pigeons whole.

Seafon them within with fpices and falt ; tie the fkin about the neck very clofe with a thread; put a piece of butter within them, and about half a fpoonful of water ; tie their feet and vent clofe up, fo that the liquor will not get out; let the gridiron be quite hot, and on a very clear fire; turn them often, to keep them from burning, until you find them thoroughly done ; be fure never to bafte any thing with butter upon the gridiron, becaufe it both fmokes and burns it ; do not cut the threads from the neck and feet till they are difh- ed ; lay them neatly in the difh, and pour beat-butter over them ; they are very juicy done in this way. When you broil the pigeons open, fplit them down the back; make the breaft as flat

as

as you can, and turn in the legs ; be
fure to fet the gridiron at a good diftance from the fire.

Difguifed Pigeons.

Seafon them with fpices and falt ;
make puffed pafte ; roll it out pretty
thick ; cut it in as many pieces as you
have pigeons ; roll the pafte about every
pigeon ; tie each of them in a cloth by
itfelf, and put them into a pot of boiling water ; they will take no more than
an hour's boiling ; take them out of
the cloths, and difh them.

A Pigeon Dumpling.

Seafon the pigeons as high as for pot-
ing ; make puffed pafte, and roll it out
round, and about an inch thick ; lay a
clean cloth in a bowl, and the pafte
above it ; put in the pigeons with their
breafts to the bottom of the bowl ; put
a piece of butter within every pigeon ;
fold the pafte round the pigeons, and
tie

tie the cloth tight about them; they
will take at leaft two hours to boil. For
all boiled puddings and dumplings, be
fure the pot is boiling before you put
them in, and turn them frequently in
the pot while boiling. For a change,
you may drefs pigeons in the fame way
as you do fried chicken. When you
cut them, blanch them a little in warm
water.

To ftew cold roafted Wild Fowl or Hare.

Cut down the wild fowl or hare in
joints; brown fome crumbs of bread in
butter; put them in to fome boiling
ftock with fome red wine; feafon it
with falt and fpices; then put in the
cold fowl or hare; let it get two or three
boils, fo as to warm it thoroughly. If
it is partridges, give it white wine in
place of red. If you have no ftock made
of beef by you, break the bones of the
meat you are cutting down, and put it
on with fome water, and an onion or
two, and draw all the ftrength out of
it. This makes a good ftock for any
hafh.

hafh of meat of any kind. You may
put in cut pickles into any hafh when a-
bout to difh them.

To ragoo Rabbits.

Cut them down in joints, and divide
the back in little pieces ; wafh them
very clean, and dry them with a cloth ;
duft them with flour, and brown them ;
thicken fome ftock with a little browned
butter and flour ; feafon it with falt and
fpices, a little wine if you choofe, the
fqueeze of a lemon, and a little ketchup.
Serve them up hot.

To ftew a Neat's Tongue whole.

Wafh it very clean with falt and water ; put it in a very clofe goblet with
as much water as will cover it ; let it
ftew for two hours ; then take it up, and
fkin it. You may add to the broth that
it boiled in a mutchkin of ftrong ftock
and a little white wine ; thicken it with
a piece of frefh butter knead in flour ;

put

put in a faggot of sweet herbs, and season it with salt and mixed spices. When
the sauce boils, put in the tongue, and
close up the pan. If it is a large tongue,
it will take two hours to stew; cut some
sellery in pieces of about an inch long;
parboil it, and put in the sauce, and let
it boil till it is tender. Some choose
carrot and turnip in it in place of sellery. When you dish it, strew in some
cut pickles; put the tongue in the middle
of the dish, pour the sauce over it, and
take out the sweet herbs.

To hash a cold Neat's Tongue.

Slice it very thin, take as much stock
as will cover it, and put some crumbs
of bread browned in butter into the
stock. When it boils, season it with
salt and spices, a little ketchup, and a
little of either red or white wine. If you
choose it, put in a few cut pickles when
you are about to dish it. Dish it on
sippets of toasted bread cut in triangular
forms, and let a little of them appear
at the side of the hash. Let no hashed
meat

meat get more boiling than warm it
thoroughly.

A Sauce for a roasted Tongue.

Slice some bread very thin; put it on
with a little water, a piece of fresh butter, some red wine, a scrape of nutmeg,
and a proper quantity of sugar; let it
boil until it is very smooth; put it in a
sauce-dish, and send it to the table,
Some choose currant-jelly in place of
wine; others choose nothing but beat-
butter and vinegar in their sauce, or
capers, if you have them.

To potch Eggs with Sorrel.

Tie up some sorrel in small faggots;
boil it; cut the strings, and lay the faggots round the dish neatly; spread them
a little, leaving a space between every
faggot; cut some toasted bread long-
ways, and put a piece between every
bunch of the sorrel; potch some eggs
very

very nicely ; take them carefully out,
and drain the water from them ; lay
them above the forrel and the bread,
allowing a little of the bread and green
tops to be feen ; beat fome frefh butter,
and pour it over them.

An Aumullete.

Take ten eggs, or a dozen if fmall ;
break and caft them, but not too much ;
put in a little fweet cream, and feafon
it with falt and a fcrape of nutmeg ;
fhred fome parfley and onions very fmall,
and mix them with the eggs ; take a
good piece of butter, let it boil a little
in a frying-pan ; pour in the eggs a-
mongft it, and fire it, but not too hafti-
ly. When it begins to faften, raife it
frequently with a knife from the bottom of the pan in different parts, to let
the butter in below it. It muft be fried
on both fides. If the ribs are clear,
hold it before the fire ; it muft not be
too hard done.

Egg

Egg and Onions, commonly called the Onion Difh.

Boil fome eggs hard ; cut fome onions in flices acrofs, and fry them with brown'd butter; take them carefully out of the butter, and drain it from them ; cut the eggs in round flices ; beat fome frefh butter; mix in fome muftard and vinegar ; then put in the eggs and onions, and tofs it upon the fire, and difh it.

CHAP. IV.

PIES, PASTIES, &c.

A Beef-fteak Pie.

TAKE a tender fat piece of beef; cut it in thin flices, and beat it well with a rolling pin ; feafon them with falt and fpices ; divide the fat pieces from the lean, and lay a fat and a lean piece together fo far as they will go ; then roll them up as you do beef collops,

collops, and pack them neatly in the dish, but don't prefs them hard ; cover it with puff'd paste, firft putting in a little water; be fure to lay a cover of the paste on the lip of the dish. Before you lay on the whole cover, dip your fingers in water, and draw them alongst the edge of the plate, before putting on the firft row of the paste ; then wet this paste in the fame manner before you lay on the cover, otherwife it would not join together.

To make a Mutton-fteak Pie.

Cut the back ribs of mutton in fingle ribs ; feafon them as in the above receipt ; lay them in the dish with a little gravy or water, as you choofe. You may put in fome potatoes and chopt fhallot. You may put fhallot into the beef-pie ; cover it in the fame way as above with ftuff'd paste.

To make a Venifon Pafty.

Bone the piece of venifon, and feafon it with black pepper and falt ; let it lie

all

all night in the feafoning; break the
bones; put them on, and draw a good
gravy from them. You may boil fome
whole pepper in it; cover the pafty-pan
with puff'd pafte; be fure to roll out
the pafte very thick; lay in the meat in
the pan, and put fome of the gravy in
with it; if the venifon is lean, take a
flap of fat mutton; let it lie all night
in fome red wine and vinegar; lay it on
the top of the venifon; then clofe it up,
and fend it to the oven : it takes a long
time of baking. When you draw it
out of the oven, fhake it. If you think
it has not enough of gravy about it,
pour in more at the top.

A mock Venifon Pafty.

Bone a fore-leg of mutton; take a
mutchkin of its own blood, and as much
claret; lay the mutton to foak in it for
twenty-four hours, and feafon it in the
fame way as the venifon pafty; lay it
into the pan, and fill it with as much
of the blood and claret it was foak'd in

as

as it will hold: it will not take fo long time of baking as the venifon one.

To make a Veal Florentine.

Cut the veal in pieces; if it is a rib piece, divide the ribs, and beat them with the chopping-knife; feafon them with falt and fpices; put a little piece of butter in the bottom of the difh, and lay in a row of the fteaks; then ftrow in fome currants and raifins above the fteaks; lay on another row of meat and fruit, until the difh is full, and put in a little water. If the veal is not very fat, lay on fome more butter on the top of it, and cover it with puff'd pafte. You may do a lamb pie the fame way. Some people do not love fweet feafoning in meat-pies; in that cafe, you may put in oyfters, the yolks of hard eggs, and arti-choke bottoms. Thefe three articles may go into all pies that have no fweet feafoning in them; but they are very good without them.

To

To make a Pigeon Pie.

Trufs the pigeons as for boiling; feafon them within with fpices and falt;
put a piece of butter into every pigeon;
put fome butter in the bottom of the
difh, and pack them in neatly. You
may fill up the vacancies between them
with the gizzards, livers, and pinions;
ftrew a little more of the feafoning over
them. In all meat-pies, remember to
put a little water or gravy in them;
cover it with puff'd pafte.

To make a Chicken Pie.

Trufs and feafon the chickens as you
do pigeons; put a piece of butter in them
and a piece in the bottom of the difh;
pack the chickens neatly in it, and ftrow
currants and raifins over them, and lay
pieces of butter above them (frefh butter is the beft;) cover it with puff'd
pafte. When it comes out of the oven,
have a caudle ready, made thus: Beat
the yolks of two eggs, and mix with them
a gill of white wine, the fame quantity
of

of cream, fome fugar, and a fcrape of
nutmeg ; make it very fmooth ; pour it
in at the top of the pie, and fhake it well.
If the chickens are very large, you may
cut them in quarters. If you don't like
them with fweet feafoning, you may
put in the yolks of hard eggs and artichoke bottoms.

To make fuperfine minced Pies.

Take the largeft neat's tongue you
can get; let it lie forty-eight hours in
falt ; then boil it ; blanch and fkin it ;
take the fineft part of the tongue, and
mince it, and four pounds of the beft
beef-fuet you can get, very fmall ; take
a pound and a half of raifins fton'd, and
cut fmall, the fame weight of currants
clean'd, half a dozen of apples pair'd, a
pound of citron, and a pound of orange-
peel cut fmall ; put them into a broad
veffel, and mix all thefe materials well
together ; beat half an ounce of Jamaica
pepper, about two drops of cloves, two
nutmegs or three according to their fize,
the grate of two large lemons, and two
or

or three tea-fpoonfuls of falt ; mix the
falt, fpices, and lemon, grate very well
together ; then feafon the minced meat
with them ; be fure to mix them until
the feafoning be all equally through
them ; then fqueeze the juice of a lemon into a mutchkin of ftrong wine,
and pour it on the minced meat ; mix
all well together ; then prefs them hard
into a can ; put a piece of white paper
clofe upon the meat, and tie paper on
the mouth of the can ; then lay them
up for ufe. If you are careful, when
you take out any of it, to prefs the remainder hard down, and paper them
well up, they will keep twelve months.
When you want to ufe them, cover the
petty-pans with puff'd pafte, and fill
them up with the minced meat ; nick
the upper cruft with a knife ; cover
them, and make them neatly up, and
fire them in the oven.

To make a common Minced Pie.

Take a tender piece of beef, according
to the fize you want the pie ; mix in

F 2   fome

fome fuet with the beef and mince both
very fine; feafon with mixed fpices and
a little falt; ftone and cut a large handful of raifins, and clean well as many
currants ; cover it with puff'd pafte as
above. It is much the better if the meat
is moiftened with a glafs or two of
wine, having a little citron and orange-
peel cut fmall put in it.

To make a Gibblet Pie.

Scald and clean the gibblets very well,
and chop the wings in two ; pull the
neck out of the fkin, and chop it in four
pieces, and cut the gizzards in pieces ;
feafon them with falt and fpices ; keep
the blood of the goofe, and ftrain it
through a fearce ; boil a few groats a
while in fweet milk ; mince fome fuet
fmall ; mix the groats and fuet with
the blood ; feafon them with falt and
fpices, and a little mint fhred fmall, if
you choofe it; fill it into the fkin of the
neck, and few up the ends of it ; turn
it round, and lay the pudding in the
middle of the difh with the gibblets
round

round it; pour in a little gravy with
them; cover with puff'd pafte, and fire
it in the oven.

To make a Hare or Muirfowl Pie.

Cut the hare in pieces; feafon it with
falt and fpices very well. If it is muir-
fowl, keep them whole, and feafon them
well within and without; lay a good
piece of butter in the bottom of the difh,
and put a piece in each of the muirfowl;
lay them in the difh with flices of butter above them; put in a little gravy or
water with them; cover them with
puff'd pafte, and fire it in the oven.
Warm a little gravy and claret; thicken
it with the yolk of an egg or two, and
pour it in at the top when the pie comes
out of the oven, and fhake it well.
Thefe pies fhould always be eat hot.
Whatever pies you fill up, always ufe
a filler; for the fauce is apt to run
over and fpoil the pafte.

To make a Kernel Pie.

Scald the kernels in boiling water;

make

make forc'd-meat balls of veal, if you
have it; it is more correspondent to
make them of veal than beef; fry them
off in the frying-pan; beat a little white
pepper and mace, the grate of a lemon,
and some salt, and season the kernels
with them; lay some fresh butter in the
bottom of the dish; put in the kernels
and balls, and cover them with puff'd
paste; warm a little white gravy, with
some white wine, the squeeze of a lemon,
and the grate of a nutmeg, and thicken
it with the yolks of eggs; pour it into
the pie when it comes out of the oven,
and shake it; put in a little gravy alongst
with the kernels. If you have plenty
of artichoke bottoms, you may put them
into any meat pies.

To make a Calf's-foot Pie.

Boil the feet tender; mince them and
some beef-suet, and some apples cut
small; season them with beat cinnamon
and nutmeg; clean and pick some currants well, and mix them all together
with a little sugar, and a glass or two of
w hite

white wine; pour on the wine, and cover
all with a good puff'd paste. The paste
ought to be nicely carved out. When
the paste is enough, the pie is ready.

A Marrow Pasty.

Blanch fix ounces of fweet almonds;
cut them very fmall; pare half a dozen
of large apples, and cut them very fmall;
cut alfo a quarter of a pound of citron
and orange peel very fmall; take three
quarters of a pound of marrow cut in
pieces. If you are fcrimped of marrow,
make it up with beef-fuet fhred very
fmall; mix all well together, and feafon
them with fugar and beat cinnamon;
cover it with puff'd pafte nicely carved
out, and fire it in the oven.

An Egg Pie.

Boil a dozen of eggs hard, and cut
them very fmall; clean about a pound
of currants; take a gill of fweet cream,
a little white wine, and a little rofe water; feafon it with beat cinnamon, fugar, and the grate of a lemon. It will
take

take three quarters of a pound of fresh
butter: mix all together, and cover it
with a carved paste as above, and fire
it in the oven.

An Eel Pie.

Skin the eels, and cut off the heads
and fins; cut them about two inches
long; season them with salt and spices;
put them into the dish with a little butter and white wine, and the juice of a
lemon; put in half a mutchkin of water, and cover it with puff'd paste.
You may make pike or trout pies in
the same way; only put more butter
in the dish with them than with eels.

A Curd Florentine.

Press the whey well from two pounds
of curds, and break them with a spoon;
beat a pound of sweet almonds with
some rose or orange-flower water; clean
half a pound of currants; cut some
boiled spinage small with a knife;
sweeten it properly; oil eight ounces of
butter, and mix all well together; make

a

a fine puff'd paſte, and lay a thin covering of it on the diſh ; then put in
the ſauce, and cover it with a carved
paſte or bard over it ; put it in a ſlow
oven ; and when the paſte is enough
baked, the florentine is ready.

An Apple Pie.

Pair and quarter the apples, and core
them ; ſeaſon them with ſugar, beat
cinnamon, and the grate of a lemon.
If you would have a very rich apple pie,
put in ſome ſton'd raiſins, blanch'd al-
mons, citron, and orange- peel cut down:
cover them with puff'd paſte. Don't
be ſparing of ſugar to any fruit pie.

An Apple Pie with Potatoes.

Boil ſome potatoes; pair and cut ſome
apples; lay a row of apples in the diſh,
and a row of potatoes above them ; then
put ſome pieces of freſh butter above the
potatoes, put apples, potatoes, and butter alternately, until the pie is filled up ;
ſweeten it to your taſte ; take rather
more apples than potatoes ; it is much
better

better of having a little citron and o-
range-peel in it ; put a little water in all
apple pies ; cover it with puff'd paste.

A Chefnut Pie.

Scald the chefnuts, and take off the
fkins ; blanch fome almonds ; pare and
quarter fome apples ; put fome frefh
butter in the bottom of the difh; lay in
a row of chefnuts, a row of apples, and
a row of almonds, with cut citron and
orange-peel, and ftrew in fugar between
the rows ; put fome more frefh butter
on the top of it, and cover it with puff'd
pafte.

A Goofeberry Pie.

Cover the difh with pafte; pick the
goofeberries, and lay them in the difh
with plenty of fugar (you can fcarcely
make a goofeberry pie too fweet), and
put in a little water: If you want it rich,
put in citron and orange-peel; cover it
with puff'd pafte. If you eat any of
thefe fruit pies cold, cut off the cover,
and pour cream over them.

To

To make Puff'd Paſte.

For one pound of flower allow three
quarters of a pound of butter ; mix in
about the fourth part of the butter a-
mongſt the flour ; wet it with cold water; then work it until it is very ſmooth ;
cut the paſte through with a knife. If
it is ſmooth in the heart, it is enough
knead ; roll it out long ways, and put
the butter on it in ſmall pieces ; then
ſhake ſome dry flour on it ; fold the
two ends of it together ; then roll it
out a little again, and put on butter
and flour as above, and continue ſo doing till all the butter is taken up; the
oftener it is folded, the more diviſions
will there be in the paſte.   Moſt people
put eggs in their puff'd paſte.   It does
very well when it is to be eat hot ; but
when eat cold, it makes it very tough
and hard.

A common Pie Paſte.

With a pound of flour mix half a
pound of butter; wet it with cold wa-

ter, and work it very fmooth : roll it
out for any ufe you intend it.

To make Pafte for the Cafes of preferved
Tarts.

Take a pound of flower; grate in a
little fugar, and mix it with fix ounces
of frefh butter; wet it with cold water;
work it very fmooth, and roll it out
equal, but not too thick; divide the
pafte, take the one half, and cut tops
for the tarts; and cut them into figures
with a pen-knife ; line the petty-pans
with the other half; prick them with
a pin, to keep them from bliftering in
the oven ; put the carved tops on crocants to fire.   If you have none, you
muft put each of them feparately on a
piece of paper ; they muft be fired in a
flow oven, elfe they will difcolour.   E-
very family fhould have fome by them,
for they keep a long time, and make a
ready difh, as you have nothing more
to do but fill them up with your preferved fruit, and lay the tops on them.
You will get crocants and cutters for the
tops

tops out of any white-iron fmiths : they are much neater and quicker than cutting with a knife.

A Pafte for raifed Pies.

For two pounds of flour take a pound of butter, and boil it in a mutchkin of water ; pour the butter and water into the flour, keeping back the fediment ; then work it up to a pafte, and before it is cold, raife it up to any fhape you pleafe.   If the pafte is not wet enough, boil a little more water and put it in.

To make Apple Tarts.

Pare fome apples ; cut them pretty fmall, and put them in as much cold water as will cover them.   If you have a piece of lemon-peel, fhred it fmall, and put it in amongft them ; let them boil until they are quite to a mafh ; turn them often in the pan ; fweeten them, and give them a boil after the fugar is in ; mix in fome beat cinnamon when they come off the fire ; and when they are cold, put them in your petty-pans,
and

and cover them with open pafte, or barred over: when the pafte is fired, they are enough.

Goofeberry Tarts.

Scald the goofeberries, but don't let them boil; then cover the petty-pans with pafte: when the berries are cold, put them in the pans with a good deal of fugar below and above them, and cover them in the fame way as the apple ones.

Cherry Tarts.

Stone the cherries; and for each pound of them take three quarters of a pound of fugar; wet it with a gill of water; boil and fcum it; then put in the cherries, and let them boil fome time; when they are cold, fill up the petty-pans, and cover them as the former.

To make Rafberry or Currant Tarts.

Pick the currants from the ftalks; put a good deal of fugar above and below them;

them ; be fure to give them loaf-fugar,
for coarfe fugar fpoils both the tafte and
colour ; cover them, and fire them in
the oven.

To make Prune Tarts.

Stew the prunes with water, claret,
and a proper quantity of fugar ; ftone
fome of them, and keep fome of them
unfton'd ; put them with the liquor
they were ftewed in into the pans ; cover them, and fire them in the oven.
You may keep out the wine, if you
choofe ; but they are much the better
of it.

Peach or Apricot Tarts.

Take the peaches or apricots before
they are quite ripe, ftone and pare them ;
you may cut them in quarters or halves ;
put a good deal of beat loaf-fugar in
the bottom of the pan ; lay in the fruit
amongft it ; ftir them often on the fire ;
let them boil a little while, and when
cold, put them into the petty pans, and
the fyrup alongſt with them ; cover
them

them with puff'd pafte, but not open in the top as the other tarts are, becaufe they take more firing.

To make a Glazing for Tarts.

Take the white of an egg and fome grated double-refined fugar; caft them very well together till it is light and white. All fine tarts fhould be glazed with it. Lay it gently on the pafte with a feather before you put them in the oven.

To make a Light Boil'd Pudding.

Take a dozen of eggs; keep out four of the whites, and caft them with fix fpoonfuls of flour quite fmooth; mix in half a pint of fweet milk; fweeten it to your tafte, and put in a little falt; feafon it with beat cinnamon and a glafs of fpirits; butter a bowl very well, and fill it full with the pudding; take a clean cloth, and butter the part that goes on the bowl very well, and drudge fome flour on it; tie the cloth very tight about the bowl; turn the mouth of the bowl undermoft undermoſt into a pot of boiling water ; be ſure the pot never goes off the boil, and it will be enough in three quarters of an hour.

A boiled Cuſtard Pudding.

Take ten eggs ; keep out ſix of the whites ; caſt them very well with ſome ſugar ; take a mutchkin and a half of ſweet cream ; ſeaſon it with beat cinnamon and the grate of a lemon ; butter a cloth or bowl ; tie it very cloſe up, and put it into a boiling pot : a quarter of an hour will boil it.

A Plumb Pudding.

Stone and ſhred a pound of raiſins ; pick and clean a pound of currants ; mince a pound of ſuet ; beat eight eggs with four ſpoonfuls of flour till it is very ſmooth ; put in a little ſalt ; ſeaſon it with cinnamon and nutmeg, and a gill of brandy ; mix all well together, and tie them up very hard ; put it in a pot of boiling water ; it will take four hours boiling.

A

A plain Suet Pudding.

Mince a pound of fuet very fmall; caft fix or feven eggs and a pound of flour; feafon it with falt, ginger, nutmeg, and a dram. If you find it very ftiff to caft, you may put a little milk in it; mix all well together; butter a cloth, and tie it up; it will take three hours boiling.

A Boiled Bread Pudding.

Cut the heart of a twopenny loaf in very thin flices; boil a chopin of milk; pour it over the bread, and cover it up for half an hour; beat ten eggs; feafon it with beat cinnamon, the grate of a lemon, if you have it, a fcrape of nutmeg, a little falt, and fugar to your tafte. You may put in fome currants and minced fuet; butter a cloth, and tie it clofe up. It will take two hours boiling, if it has fuet and currants in it; if without them, only an hour and an half. If you intend it for a fide affet,

half

half the quantity will do it, and it will
take lefs boiling.

A boiled Rice Pudding.

Take a quarter of a pound of rice,
and put it on with a chopin of cold milk
and a good piece of frefh butter ; keep
it clofe ftirring on the fire till it boils :
if you find it not very thick, ftir in fome
more rice till it is like thick pottage ;
caft fix eggs ; mix them very well with
the rice and milk, and fweeten it to
your tafte ; put in a very little falt ;
feafon it with cinnamon and nutmeg,
the grate of a lemon, and a dram ; butter a cloth, and tie it up clofe ; it will
take an hour to boil.

The proper fauce for all boiled puddings is frefh butter beat with wine
and fugar. When you butter a cloth
to boil a pudding in, dredge a little
flour over the butter. You will obferve,
in the boiling of all puddings, that the
pot muft be kept full of water, and never allow it to go off the boil ; turn the
pudding frequently in the pot, efpeci-
a'ly

ally at the beginning, till the pudding is well faftened.

A Peafe Pudding.

Take a pound of fplit peafe, or more as you have occafion; tie them up in a cloth not too clofe, that they may have room to fwell ; let them boil an hour ; then take them up and mix a good piece of butter in them, and tie them up hard ; they will take near another hour's boiling ; divide the pudding in two, and lay the pork in the middle. Send beat-butter along with them to the table.

A whole Rice Pudding.

Take half a pound of rice; wafh it well in water, and boil it in a chopin of fweet milk till it is almoft dry, ftirring it on the fire to keep it from burning ; ftir in fix ounces of frefh butter; let it cool a little ; caft five or fix eggs; mix with them about a gill of fweet cream ; them mix all together ; feafon with cinnamon, nutmeg, fugar, and a dram ;

dram; ftone and clean half a pound of currants and raifins, and put them in. In all baked puddings, be fure to rub a little butter on the difh before you put it in. Garnifh all baked puddings with puffed pafte in any figure you choofe.

Another Rice Pudding.

Take the flour of rice, and boil it in the fame way as you do the boiled rice pudding; beat five eggs and mix them with the rice and milk; fweeten it to your tafte; feafon it pretty high with the grate of oranges. If you have not this, feafon it with any fpice you pleafe, and give it a dram; but when it is high flavoured with the oranges, it needs no dram; put it in the oven.

A Lair Pudding.

Beat eight eggs; keep out four of the whites; mix in a mutchkin of fweet milk, and fweeten it to your tafte; feafon it with cinnamon, nutmeg, and a dram; cut fome very thin flices of a
loaf

loaf of fine bread; dry it before the
fire, or in an oven; it muſt not be
brown; have ſome ſuet finely ſhred,
ſome currants and raiſins ſtoned and
cleaned; lay a row of ſuet in the bottom
of the diſh; then break the dried bread
in pieces, and put a row of it above the
ſuet, then a row of fruit; take the milk
and eggs, and put it over the bread in
ſpoonfuls till the bread is moiſtened
with it; then begin again with a row of
ſuet, bread, and fruit, until the diſh is
full, and put in as much of the eggs
and milk as the diſh will admit of; it
ſhould ſoak an hour before you put it
in the oven; and as the bread ſucks up
the cuſtard, add more until the plate is
quite full; it takes very little firing, for
when the cuſtard is curdled it is not
good; when the milk and eggs are well
faſtened, it is enough.

A Marrow Pudding.

Grate the crumbs of a twopenny
loaf; boil three mutchkins of ſweet
cream, and pour it boiling hot on the
grated

grated bread; beat fix eggs; cut a pound of marrow in pieces, not too fmall; ftone and clean fome currants and raifins; fweeten it to your tafte, and feafon it with cinnamon and nutmeg; mix all thefe materials well together, and put them in a difh. If you have not marrow, good beef-fuet does very well; but it muft be minced very fine. If you want this or any of the boiled puddings to appear yellow, fteep fome faffron in a little milk, or dram, or rofe water, and mix it in the pudding; put it in the oven and fire it.

A Tanfy Pudding.

Cut thin flices of fine bread; boil fome cream, and pour it boiling on the bread; cover it up till the bread has fucked up all the cream; beat ten eggs, and keep out four of the whites; mix them in with the bread, and fweeten it to your tafte; beat fome tanfy, and fqueeze out the juice through a clean cloth; put in as much of it as make it bitter to your tafte; put in fome of the

juice

juice of fpinage with it to make it of a
fine green ; put in a dram, the fcrape of
a nutmeg, and four ounces of frefh butter; put all into a pan, and give it a beat
on the fire till it is pretty thick ; then
put it into a pudding-pan, and fire it
off in the oven. When you are to fend
it to the table, ftrew fugar on the top,
and fliced orange. If you make it with
milk inftead of cream, you muft put a
great deal more butter in it.

An Orange Pudding.

Take the yolks of a dozen of eggs;
beat and fift half a pound of fugar ; put
it in by degrees, and caft it amongft the
eggs with a knife ; it muft be caft until they are thick and white. If you
have the conferve of oranges, put in as
much of it as give it a fine tafte, and
caft it along with the eggs. If you have
not this, put fome beat marmalade in
place of it.   Beat two ounces of fugar-
bifcuit; mix all well together, and you
muft caft it conftantly until it goes into
the oven, or it won't be light ; juft when
it

it is ready to go into the oven, pour in
five or fix ounces of fresh butter oiled,
but do not let it be too hot when you
put it in ; mix all well together, and put
it in the oven.

A Lemon Pudding.

Grate the rhind of three or four lemons, and lay it to fteep in a gill of
brandy ; beat the yolk of ten or twelve
eggs, as in the above receipt, with the
fame quantity of fugar, bifcuit, and
butter. You muft order it every way
as in the orange pudding ; all the difference is in the feafoning, the one lemon
and the other orange ; and wherever
orange grate is, it needs no fpirits to
raife it.

A Citron Pudding.

Slice half a pound of citron thin, and
fhred it very fmall with a knife ; beat
and fift half a pound of fugar ; beat the
citron and fugar very well together in a
marble mortar ; have the yolks of ten
or a dozen of eggs caft, until they are
G like

like a cream; then mix them by degrees into the beat sugar and citron, and caſt them very well with a ſpoon or a knife. You may mix in a very little ſugar-biſcuit. Put in as much of the juice of ſpinage as make it of a fine green; mix all well together. When you are juſt about putting it into the oven, put in a dram and oiled butter, and mix it very well. In all fine baked puddings, let the oiled butter be the laſt thing you put in, and let it not be too hot. You may make a lemon pudding little inferior to a citron one, by putting in a good piece of citron cut very ſmall amongſt it, and green it with the juice of ſpinage.

A Green Gooſeberry Pudding.

Put on a pint of gooſeberries with a very little water; let them boil to a maſh, and thruſt them through a ſearce with the back of a ſpoon; beat ten eggs, keeping out ſix of the whites; then take all the fine pulp of the gooſeberries that comes through the ſearce, and beat

up

up with the eggs, and half a pound of
fugar. If it is not fweet enough, put in
more. You may mix in it fome citron
and orange-peel cut fmall, with a quarter of a pound of fugar-bifcuit. Juft
when you are about to put it in the
oven, pour in the oiled butter, and mix
all well together.

An Apple Pudding.

Roaft feven or eight large apples; take
the fkins off, and fcrape out all the pulp;
beat the fame quantity of eggs, and all
the other materials, as in the foregoing
receipt. Thefe two puddings you may
green with fpinage-juice, as they look
the better of it.

An Almond Pudding.

Blanch half a pound of fweet almonds
and a few bitter ones ; beat them very
fine, fo that they will fpread on your
fingers like a pafte ; be fure as you beat
to wet them with fome brandy ; beat
the yolks of ten or a dozen of eggs, with
half a pound of fugar beat and fifted ;
caft

caft them till they are light and white..
You may put in about an ounce of beat
bifcuit, and feafon it with the grate of
orange or lemon, if you have it, and
fome oiled butter.

A Sago or Millet Pudding.

Put on the fago with a chopin of water, a ftick of cinnamon, and the rhind
of a lemon ; let it boil till it is pretty
thick ; put in half a mutchkin of white
wine, and fugar to your tafte ; beat fix
eggs well, keeping out half of the
whites ; mix all well together. You
may make a millet pudding the fame
way ; only boil the millet in milk, and
give it two or three eggs more, and give
it a dram in place of wine ; let them be
pretty cold before you mix in the eggs
and oiled butter.

A Potatoe Pudding.

When the potatoes are boiled and
fkinned, take half a pound of the beft
of them, and beat them very well in a
mortar : beat nine eggs, and, keep out
three

three of the whites; caft them thick
with half a pound of fugar; mix in
with the potatoes half a mutchkin of
cream; then caft them up well together
with the fugar and eggs; feafon it with
cinnamon and nutmeg, and give it a
good dram; it will take half a pound
of oiled butter at leaft.

*A common Potatoe Pudding to be fired below
roafted meat.*

Boil and fkin as many potatoes as will
fill the difh; beat them, and mix in
fome fweet milk; put them on the fire
with a good piece of butter; feafon them
properly with falt and fpices. Some
choofe an onion fhred fmall, and put in
it. Put it in the difh and fire it below
the meat, until it is of a fine brown on
the top; caft three eggs well, and mix
in with the potatoes before you put them
in the difh; it makes it rife, and eat
light; pour off all the fat that drops
from the meat, before you fend it to
the table: it eats very well with roafted
beef or mutton

A

A Bread Pudding to be fired below meat.

Take a chopin of milk, and flice down as much of the heart of a fine loaf as make it very thick ; put it on the fire and boil it. If you fee it too thin of bread, put in a little more ; let it boil until it is pretty thick, ftirring it from the bottom of the pan to keep it from burning ; put in a handful of fuet ; if you have none, put in a piece of frefh butter ; take it off the fire, and fweeten it to your tafte ; feafon it with what fpices you choofe ; beat fix eggs, and let the pudding be a little cold before you put them in ; mix all well together, and put it into a difh, and fire it below the meat ; turn the difh often, to make it of an equal brown ; pour off all the fat before you fend it to the table.

A Hafty Pudding.

Order as much bread and milk, and in the fame way as in the above receipt, as will fill a fmall bowel to fit an affet ;

put

put in a piece of frefh butter ; pick and
clean a handful of currants, and boil
them alongft with the bread and milk ;
caft four eggs, and put in it ; feafon it
with cinnamon, nutmeg, and fugar ;
after the eggs are in, ftir it a while on
the fire to faften it, but don't let it come
a-boil ; then butter a bowl very well,
and put the pudding in it ; fet it before
the fire, or in a white-iron oven, turning the bowl often. If the fire is pretty
hot, it will very foon faften ; turn it out
of the bowl into an affet, and fend up
to the table the fame fauce as for the
former boiled puddings.

A Carrot Pudding.

Boil fome good carrots ; and when
they are well clean'd, weigh half a pound
of them ; beat them very fine in a mortar ; mix two or three fpoonfuls of
fweet cream along with them ; beat ten
eggs (keep out half of the whites) with
half a pound of fugar ; mix all well together, and feafon it with beat cinnamon, or orange grate, if you have it, as
it

it makes it eat like an orange pudding ;
mix eight ounces of oil'd butter in it,
juſt when you are about putting it into
the oven.

An Apple Dumpling.

Make a good puff'd paſte ; roll it out
about half an inch thick ; pair the apples, and cut them down very ſmall ;
then butter a ,cloth, and put it into a
bowel ; lay the paſte in it, and put in
the apples, wrap the paſte about the
apples, and tie the cloth hard up. If it
is a large one, it will take three hours
boiling ; if a little one, leſs time will do
it.   You may make any fruit dumpling
in the ſame way ; currants, cherries.
raſberries, apricots, or any fruit you
pleaſe.   Moſt people don't ſweeten them
until after they come out of the pot ; but
I always found it better to ſweeten them
before I put them in ; for the ſugar always incorporates better w th the fruit.
If it is an apple dumpling, cut out a
piece of the paſte at the top, and put in

a piece of frefh butter, and lay on the piece again.

Sir Robert Walpole's Dumplings.

Take a pound of fuet; fhred it fmall; grate fome ftale bread, till you have a-bout three quarters of a pound; pick and clean about a pound of currants; cut a quarter of a pound of orange-peel and citron fmall; mix all together, and feafon it with cinnamon and fugar; caft fix or eight eggs, and keep out half of the whites; mix in the eggs with the other ingredients, and a dram; it muft be no more than wet with the eggs, to to make it ftick like a pafte. You fhould have fmall nets, wrought of fmall pack-thread; put in every one into a net, until they are about the fize of a good large apple; tie them clofe in the net; make them all of one fize, except one for the middle, make it a little larger; put them into a pot of boiling water; they will take about an hour's boiling. If you have no nets, you may tie them up in pieces of clean rags; difh them, and

pour

pour beat butter, wine, and fugar over them.

To make Curd-cheefe Cakes.

Earn two pints of milk; put it on the back of a fearce, and let the whey drain from it: when it is well drain'd, beat the curd in a mortar; beat a quarter of a pound of fugar-bifcuit; mix it with the curd, and fweeten it to your tafte; beat four eggs; have half a pound of currants pick'd and cleaned; caft them all well up together; feafon them with cinnamon and orange-grate, and a dram in fix ounces of oil'd frefh butter; beat them all well together; have fome petty-pans covered with puff'd pafte; put in the cheefe-cake meat, but don't fill the pans too full; glaze them over with a beat egg and fugar; cut the pafte with a runner like ftraws, and ornament the tops with them in any figure you pleafe; put them in the oven, and fire them.

To

To make Lemon Cheese-cakes.

Boil the skins of three lemons until they are as tender as they will be ; but take off the grate before you boil them : beat them very fine with half a pound of fine sugar ; beat six eggs, but keep out the half of the whites ; cast them until they are light and white ; mix them very well ; season them with le-mon-grate and cinnamon ; put in a little brandy, and fix ounces of oiled butter.   After mixing all well together, put them in the petty-pans, but don't fill them near full, and fire them in the oven.

To make Almond Cheese-cakes.

Blanch and beat half a pound of al-monds ; wet them with a little brandy while you are beating them ; cast six eggs (keeping out four of the whites) with fine sugar, and cast all together with the almonds; season them with the grate of lemons or oranges ; put in fix ounces of oil'd fresh butter ; mix all well

well together; put them in the petty-
pans, and fire them in the oven.

To make Cuſtards.

Take a mutchkin of good ſweet cream;
put it on the fire with a ſtick of cinnamon and lemon-peel; let them boil until the ſtrength is out of the cinnamon,
ſtirring it always one way to keep it
from bratting; caſt the yolks of eight
eggs till they are very light and ſmooth;
mix them with a gill of cold cream;
then mix them by degrees with the
boil'd cream; take out the cinnamon
and lemon-peel, and ſweeten the cream
to your taſte; put them into cûps, and
fire them. You may put a little wine in
them, if you chooſe it.

To make Rice Cuſtards.

Boil a mutchkin of ſweet milk with
two ounces of freſh butter; put in two
ounces of the flower of rice with the cold
milk, and let them boil for a little time
together; beat two eggs, and mix them
with the boil'd milk and rice; ſtir them
on

on the fire until they thicken, but don't let them boil ; feafon them with the grate of an orange and fugar ; then put them into cups.

To make Almond Cuftards.

Put on a mutchkin of cream with cinnamon and lemon-peel, as in the former cuftards, the fame quantity of eggs, mixed in the fame way with the cold cream ; blanch and beat a quarter of a pound of almonds ; wet them with a little rofe-water as you beat them ; then mix them with the eggs ; mix the warm cream and them altogether by degrees, and fweeten them to your tafte ; put them on the fire again, keeping them ftirring one way ; but don't let milk or eggs ever come to a-boil ; put them into cups, and fire them. You may fire all cuftards in a flow oven, or you may put the cups into a panful of cold water ; put the pan on the fire, and cover it ; take care the water is not fo high as to boil into the cups. When you fee them faftened, they are enough.

To

To make clear Lemon Cream.

Pare four large lemons very thin ; lay the parings into half a mutchkin of water ; fqueeze the juice of the lemons into it, and let it ftand one night ; ftrain it off, and boil it up with a pound of double refined fugar and a gill of rofe-water ; fcum it very well, and take the whites of nine eggs. You muft not whip them too much, elfe they will frothe ; ftrain the whites through a fearce, and mix them with the liquor by degrees, for fear of curdling ; put it on a very clear fire, ftirring it one way ; let it be fcalding hot, and put it into glaffes. There is no difference between this and the yellow lemon cream ; only beat in two of the yolks alongft with the whites, and put it into a china difh.

To make an Orange Cream.

Pare the rhind off three bitter oran-ges ; lay it in half a mutchkin of wa-ter ; let it lye until it has a fine flavour of the rhind ; fqueeze the juice of the

oranges

oranges into it; ftrain it off, and boil it up with half a pound of double refined fugar; caft the yolks of fix eggs with the fugar, and mix in the liquor by degrees; fet it on the fire, and ftir it one way until it is fcalding hot. You may put it into cups, glaffes, or a china affet.

To make Ratafia Cream.

Boil four laurel bay leaves in a chopin of cream; beat the yolks of fix eggs; keep out a little of the cream when cold, and mix it with the beat eggs; then mix in the warm cream amongft the eggs by degrees; put it on the fire, and keep it ftirring one way; let it be fcalding hot, but not boiling: take out the leaves, and fweeten it to your tafte. If you have not laurel bay leaves, blanch and beat a few bitter almonds: wet them with a little cream as you beat them, to keep them from oiling; mix the cold cream with the almonds; thruft them through a fcarce, and mix them in with the eggs.

To

To make Sweet Almond Cream.

Boil a chopin of cream with cinnamon and lemon peel ; blanch and beat
half a pound of sweet almonds ; wet
them with a little rose water, as you
beat them ; beat the whites of eight
eggs very well ; mix them with the almonds, and thrust them through a
searce ; mix in the boil'd cream gradually amongst them, and put them on
the fire, stirring it one way ; make it
scalding hot, but don't let it boil; sweet-
en it to your taste, taking out the stick
of cinnamon and the lemon peel. You
may put these two creams either into
cups or china dishes.

To make Clouted Cream.

Take four pints of new milk ; set it
on a clear fire, and stir it now and
then : whenever it comes a boil take it
off, and put it into broad dishes to cool;
stir it about in the dishes for some time
after it is turned out of the pan; set it
in a cool place, and let it stand twenty-
four

four hours; then fcum off the clouts with a fkimmer, and lay it on the difh; put fweet cream about it, and ftrew cinnamon and fugar over it. Spanifh cream is made of the brats thus: Take the brats, and beat them well in a bowl with a fpoon, with fome fine fugar and a little rofe-water; it muft be beat until it is very thick. You may difh it, with fome fweat cream about it. If you have plenty of brats, you may lay a row of them and a row of the Spanifh cream time about.

To make Velvet Cream.

Take a little fyrup, of either lemons or oranges, or any kind of fyrup you have; put two or three fpoonfuls of it in the bottom of a difh; warm fome new milk lukewarm; pour the milk on the fyrup, and put in as much runnet as will faften it, and cover it up with a plate.

To make Steeple Cream.

Take a chopin of fweet cream and
two

two pints of new milk; set it on the
fire to come a-boil, and stir it to keep
it from bratting; turn it into dishes to
cool; then scum off the top, and put
it on to boil again, and so continue to
boil, cool, and scum, until you have
a good quantity of the cream. Just
when you are going to whisk it, put in
half a mutchkin of Lisbon or Zerry, the
juice of a lemon, and as much fine sugar beat and sifted as will sweeten it to
your taste; whisk it up until it is very
thick; raise it up as high as you can
in the asset, in the shape of a sugar-
loaf.

To make Bandstring Curd.

Earn some new milk; press the whey
very well out of it; put it into a squirt
that has small holes in it, and squirt it
into the asset; it looks just like band-
strings; put fine sugar and sweet cream
over it.

Rush Curd.

Wash some green rushes very clean;
cut

cut them about a quarter long, and lay
them round ways on the back of a
hair fearce ; earn about five chopins of
new milk ; take up the curd in flices
with a fkimming-difh, and lay it on
the rufhes to drain the whey from it,
and as the whey is drain'd, lay on more
of the curds, until it is all on ; let it
ftand for an hour or two, and by that
time the whey will be well drain'd from
it ; lay the difh you intend to ferve it
up in on the top of the curd, and turn
the fearce upfide down, and take the
rufhes off the curd. It is eat with fugar
and cream ; but fend the cream in a
bowl to the table.

Tender Curd.

Earn the milk and prefs the whey
well from it ; beat it very well in a
mortar with a little fine fugar, then
prefs it hard into tea-cups, or into any
fhape you pleafe ; when it is well faftened in the fhapes, turn it out on an affet, and pour fweet cream over it. All
thefe curds muft be made of milk newly-
ly

ly taken from the cow, elfe they will
not eat well. You may garnifh all milk
difhes with any kind of fweet-meats you
have.

To make Fairy Butter.

Take the yolks of three hard eggs,
four ounces of loaf-fugar, fix ounces of
frefh butter, as new from the churn as
you can, and two fpoonfuls of orange
flower or rofe-water; beat them all very
well until they are like pafte; then put
it into a fqnirt, and fqui.t it on an affet
in little heaps.

Syllabubs.

Take half a mutchkin of fweet cream,
half a mutchkin of white wine, and the
juice of a lemon; fweeten it to your
tafte with fine fugar; put in a bit of
the paring of a lemon, and a piece of
cinnamon, if you choofe; whifk it very
well, and as it rifes take it up with a
fpoon, and lay it on the back of a fearce
to drain the whey from it; then fill
the glaffes half full of wine, and fweeten
it;

it; then fill up the glaffes with the whifked cream; lay as much on the glaffes as will ftand on it.

Another kind of Syllabubs.

Take a chopin of thick cream; put in it three gills of white wine, the juice of a lemon, the juice of two bitter oranges, and fugar; beat them very well till you fee it thick; then fcum it with a fpoon, and fill up the glaffes. You put in a piece of cinnamon and lemon-peel as in the former; but be fure you take them out before you put it into the glaffes.

Bla mange.

Break down half an ounce of ifin-glafs; put it on with a gill of water; put it on and off the fire until it is dif-folved; add to it a chopin of very fwet cream that will bear boiling; for if it break, it is fpoiled; put in a piece of the rhind of a lemon and a ftick of cinnamon; let all boil together for fome time. If you like it with the ratafa

taíte,

tafte, blanch and beat a very few bitter
almonds, and boil along with it; fweeten
it to your tafte, and ftrain it through a
fearce ; be fure to ftir it on the fire, o-
therwife it will brat after it is ftrained.
You muft ftir it until it is quite cold before you put it into any fhape, or elfe
the cream will fly to the top and the
ifinglafs to the bottom.   When it is
thorough faftened, put the fhape into
hot water to loofe the blanmange from
it, and turn it out on an affet as quick
as you can.   Turn out every other jelly
in the fame way.

Goofeberry Cream.

Boil fome goofeberries until they are
fo foft that a fpoon can thurft them
through the back of a fearce ; take the
pulp that comes through the fearce ; feparate it from the feeds, and fweeten it
to your tafte ; mix it up with thick
fweet cream, and put it on an affet. You
may make apple cream in the fame way.

To

To make Strawberry, Rasberry, or Currant Cream.

If the fruit is new pulled, take equal weight of sugar and fruit; clarify the sugar, and put in the fruit: let them boil until the sugar has penetrated into the heart of the fruit; and when cold, take two or three spoonfuls of it; whisk it up with a mutchkin of th' *·* cream; then take the wholeft of the berries, and mix in two or three spoonfuls more amongst the whisk'd cream. You may either put it into an affet or glasses. If you have any of those fruits preserved, you may do them in the same way.

To make Rice Cream.

Take three spoonfuls of the flour of rice, and put it on with a mutchkin of sweet cream, and stir it until it comes a-boil; then let it cool; cast the yolks of three eggs with sugar, and mix a little cold milk or cream with them; then mix it with the rice, and keep it stirring one way; but take care it does not boil.

You

You may flavour it either with orange-flower water or rofe-water. If you have none of thefe, boil a piece of cinnamon along with the rice ; difh it, and fend it cold to the table.

A rich Eating-poffet.

Take a chopin of fweet cream, half a pound of common bifcuit beat and fearced ; blanch fix ounces of fweet almonds ; beat them up with a little fweet milk to keep them from oiling; mix the cream, almonds, and bifcuit together ; put them into a pan, and let them boil a while ; take a mutchkin of white wine, and caft nine eggs, keeping out fix of the whites, and add them to the wine, and fweeten it to your tafte ; feafon it with beat cinnamon ; put the wine and eggs on the fire, and let them come a-boil ; then put them into a bowl ; pour the cream on the wine, and ftir it about; put fugar and cinnamon on the top. It looks very pretty ftuck with fliced almonds on the top ; it goes to the table
in

in a bowl; it is a proper middle difh·
for fupper.

A common Eating-poffet.

Take a bottle of good ale and a mutchkin of wine; put it in, and warm it
with a little beat cinnamon; fweeten it;
toaft fome thin flices of bread; cut it in
dices, and put it amongft the wine; boil
three mutchkins of new milk, and pour
it boiling hot on the bread and wine;
ftir it all about with a fpoon, and cover
it up; fend it hot to the table, either in
a bowl or a foup difh. It is a very
good fupper-difh.

To make Hartfhorn Jelly.

Put on two pints of water in a clofe
goblet with a pound of hartfhorn; let it
boil on a flow fire until half of the water is wafted; you put in half an ounce
of ifinglafs alongft with the hartfhorn;
lift a little of it in a fpoon, and let it
cool, that you may fee the ftiffnefs of it.
If it is ftiff enough, ftrain it off; if not,
let it boil a little longer.———With re-

H   gard

gard to feafoning, I can give no rule,
but to fweeten it ; put in wine and the
juice of lemons to your tafte, a little of
the rhind of lemon, a good piece of cinnamon broke in bits ; caft the whites of
four or fix eggs, according to the quantity ; break fome of the egg-fhells a-
mongft the whites ; mix all together ;
put it on the fire, and keep it ftirring
and fkinking, not to let the eggs turn
to a hat ; let it boil until the ftrength is
out of the cinnamon ; then turn it into
the jelly-bag ; have two bowls ready to
receive it ; turn it backwards and forwards into the bag, until you fee it
clear, fit for glaffes.

Calves-feet Jelly.

Put four calves feet into a pot with
water ; fcald them, and take the hair very
clean off them ; flit them, and lay them
into warm water ; let them blanch two
hours ; fet them on in a very clofe pan
with two pints of water on a flow fire ;
let them boil to rags ; then ftrain them
off, and fcum all the fat off the ftock.
When

When it is quite cold, cut off all the fediment from the bottom. It is feafoned every way as the hartfhorn jelly is. If
you are careful of turning it often into
the bag, it will be as clear as the hartfhorn jelly. If the ftock is very ftiff,
put in fome water in it; it is not pretty
to be ftiff in glaffes; but if it is for a
fhape, it muft be a great deal ftiffer, or
elfe it will not ftand when you turn it
out.

Jelly for a Confumption.

Take a pound of hartfhorn fhavings,
nine ounces of eringo root, three ounces
of ifinglafs, a chopin of bruifed fnails,
the fhells taken off and clean'd; take
two vipers, or four ounces of the powder
of them; put all thefe ingredients in
two Scotch pints of water, and let them
boil into one pint; ftrain it through a
fearce; when it is cold, put it into a
pan with a mutchkin of Rhenifh wine,
half a pound of brown fugar-candy, the
juice of two Seville oranges, and the
whites of three or four eggs well beat;
boil

boil them altogether for three or four
minutes; then run it through a jelly-
bag, and put it into fmall pots. The
patient may take two tea-cupfuls of it
in a day,

A Hen's Neft.

Make a ftrong jelly of calves feet or
hartfhorn; take a bowl, the mouth of
which will go within the affet you intend to difh it on; fill about a third
part of the bowl with the jelly when it
is cold and firm; lay in the eggs; melt
down the reft of the jelly, and let it be
quite cold, but not faftened, and pour it
on the eggs; take the thin pairings of
lemons, and boil them a little in water;
cut them like ftraws, and ftrew them on
the top of the jelly before it is quite
firm. You make the eggs of blanmange.

Jelly in Cream.

Fill fmall cups full of the jelly; when
it is firm, turn the cups out upon a
china affet, and put fome thick fweet
cream

cream round the jelly in the bottom of the affet. This way of making up jelly looks very well, efpecially when it is on a pretty difh, as the painting is very beautiful through the jelly.

To difh up cold Chicken in Jelly.

Lay the jelly in the bottom of a bowl as you do in the hen's neft; take a cold roafted chicken or two, if the bowl will hold them; turn their breafts down to the bottom of the bowl, and drop the yolks of fome hard eggs in amongft the jelly round the chickens; then fill up the bowl with the jelly; let it ftand until it is firm; then turn it out. It muft not be feafoned as the other jellies are. Boil in the ftock a little white pepper, a blade of mace, a bit of lemon-peel, and the fqueeze of a lemon, and a very little falt; clarify it as the former jelly, and run it through a jelly-bag in the fame manner. You may garnifh with any thing that is green.

A Floating Island.

Roaft fome apples ; toaft off the fkins, and take out the pulp, and caft it very well with a knife with the white of an egg and fugar, until it is very light and white; take half a pound of currant jelly and four whites of eggs ; whifk it up with the whifk all one way, till it is fo thick, that when you drop it from the fpoon it will ftand ; it takes a long time whifking until it is of a proper ftiffnefs; put fome fweet cream in the bottom of a difh ; cover the cream with the roafted apples, and drop on the jelly in what figure you pleafe ; raife the apples and jelly as high in the middle as you can. You may do it without apples ; but it takes a great deal more jelly to cover the cream.

A Trifle.

Take fome white wine and fugar ; dip fome fugar-bifcuit in it ; lay the bifcuit in the bottom of a difh, and bring it by degrees to be high in the middle ;

middle; when the bifcuit is a little
foftened with the wine, pour fome thick
fweet cream over it ; let it ftand until
the bread has fuck'd up the wine and
the cream : if there is any of the liquor
left, pour it off.   If you have apples,
roaft fome of them, and order them in
the fame way as in the laft receipt ; lay
a covering of apples on the bifcuit ;
then cover it all over with whipt cream,
and drop fome currant-jelly on it.   In
cafe you have not fweet cream, put on
fome fweet milk with a bit of cinnamon
and lemon-peel ; let it boil ; take the
yolks of four eggs to a mutchkin of
milk ; caft them until they are very
fmooth, and mix them up with a little
cold milk ; then mix the boiling milk
by degrees amongft the eggs, and turn
it backwards and forwards until it is
very fmooth ; then put it on the fire a
little ; keep it ftirring, but don't let it
boil.   This fupplies the place of real
cream when you have none ; fweeten it
to your tafte.

An

An Egg Cheefe.

Take three mutchkins of fweet cream not too thick ; put it on with a little cinnamon, lemon-peel, fugar, and half a mutchkin of white wine ; caft a dozen of eggs ; keep out fix of the whites ; mix the eggs very well with the cold milk ; put it on the fire, and keep it ftirring all the time until it comes a-boil. When you fee it is broke, turn it into any fhape you have with holes, to let it ftand until the whey runs from it, and turn it out of the fhape. You may flavour it either with orange-flower or rofe-water before you put it into the fhape. If you choofe, you may pour fweet cream over it when you difh it, or it may be eat with wine and fugar.

To make a Cheefe Loaf.

Take three chopins of new milk ; put in as much runnet as will make it cur-dle ; prefs the whey gently from the curd ; break the curd, and take equal quantity

quantity of grated bread and curd; beat the yolks of a dozen of eggs and fix of the whites; feafon with beat cinnamon, nutmeg, and fugar; mix in half a mutchkin of fweet cream and a glafs of brandy; mix the bread and curd all together, and put a very little falt in it; work it all up to a pafte, and duft in two or three fpoonfuls of flour as you work it up; take out a piece of it, and roll it out thin to fry; then make the reft up in the fhape of a loaf, and fire it in the oven; cut the fried pafte in little bits to put round the loaf; cut a hole in the top of the loaf, and pour in fome beat butter, cream, and fugar; fend it hot to the table.

To make fine Pan-cakes.

For every two eggs take a fpoonful of flour; beat the flour and eggs until they are quite fmooth; fweeten it; put in beat cinnamon, a very little falt, and a dram; for every fix eggs mix in a mutchkin of fweet cream; oil fix ounces of frefh butter; mix it in with the batter

ter; put butter in the frying-pan at
firſt; let the pan be very hot, and put
in a tea-cupful of the batter at a time
in the pan, and turn the pan round to
make it of an equal thicknefs.   If you
think it too thin, put a little more batter in the pan; when it is fired on that
fide, you muſt hold the other fide before the fire; for thefe light pan-cakes
will not turn; double it in the pan;
then fold it again; lift it with a knife,
and lay it on a warm plate before the
fire to keep it hot; be fure that the pan
is quite hot every cake you put in; ſtir
always the batter before you put it into
the pan.

To make a very good baked Pudding with
the fame Batter.

Butter a pudding-pan; put in the
batter, and fire it in an oven; it will
rife very light in the oven.   When you
fee the butter all fuck'd up, and the
pudding begins to grow brown, it is
enough.

To

To turn the fame Batter into a different form.

Butter fome tea-cups, and fill them more than half full; fire them in the oven; when enough, turn them out of the cups on a plate. Send beat-butter, wine, and fugar, to eat with thefe puddings.

To make Pan-puddings.

Beat four or five eggs with four fpoonfuls of flour; caft it until the flour is free of knots; put in a little falt and fugar to your tafte, beat cinnamon and nutmeg, near a mutchkin of fweet milk, a dram, a handful of currants, and as much fweet fuet fhred fmall; mix all well together; put a piece of butter in the frying-pan, or beef-dripings : when it boils, lay as many petty-pans in the frying-pan as it will hold, with their bottoms upmoft; put in the pudding-ftuff at the bottom of the petty-pans. You muft fry them on a flow fire, otherwife you will burn

H 6 them,

them, and they will be raw in the heart. When the petty-pans come eafily off, they are ready for turning to the other fide. They eat well, and are a very pretty difh.

To make Apple Fritters.

Beat four or five eggs; mix in as much flour as they will caft with till they are very fmooth; put in a little falt, fugar, and fome beat ginger; you may put in cinnamon, if you choofe; mix in about a gill of fweet cream or new milk; two or three fpoonfuls of fweet yeft; caft them all well together; put down the batter at a diftance before the fire to make it rife. If you have not yeft, you muft give it a good dram. Pare the apples, and cut them in thin flices; take out the cores, but keep the flices whole; have a good deal of beef-drippings boiling in the pan; then put in every flice of the apples by itfelf a-mongft the batter, and drop them into the pan one by one until it is full; fry them a light brown; take them carefully

ly from the fat, and keep them warm
before the fire till they are all fried off;
then dish them neatly one above another; raise them pretty high in the middle, and strew sugar over them. Send
them hot to the table.

To make Currant Fritters.

Make the batter in the same way as
in the former; put in a quarter of a
pound of currants well wash'd and dried.
If you have any beef-suet, shred a little
of it small, and put amongst it; mix all
well together, and drop them from a
spoon into the frying-pan into what size
you please. Dish them in the same way
as the above.

To make Oyster Fritters.

Make the batter in the same way as
in the above receipts; only keep out
the sugar and cinnamon; pickle the
oysters; take as many of them as you
want, and lay them between the folds
of a cloth, and dry them; then dip
every oyster in the batter, and fry them
in

in the same way as the other fritters; dish them hot, but put no sugar on them.

To make Potatoe Fritters.

Boil and beat half a dozen of potatoes; mix them with four beat eggs, about a gill of good thick cream, some sugar and nutmeg, a little salt, a bit of fresh butter oiled, and a dram; beat them all well together, and drop them in the boiling drippings; fry them a light brown; dish them hot, and strew sugar over them.

You may put *any preserved fruit* in the heart of fritters, such as, preserved cherries or gooseberries, or the half of an appricot; be sure to have a great deal of fat to fry all fritters in, else they will not be good. Some choose their apples chopt small, and mixed in the batter in place of slices.

To make a Tansy Cake.

Beat six eggs with four or five spoonfuls

fuls of flour; mix with them a mutchkin of fweet cream or new milk; fweet-
en it to your tafte; feafon it with fome
nutmeg and a little falt; put in as much
of the juice of tanfy as bitter it to your
tafte, and make it green with the juice
of fpinage; mix fome oiled butter in it,
and caft them all well together; you
may fire it in a frying-pan on the top of
the fire, but take care not to burn it.
You may fire it below meat that is roaft-
ing, or in an oven; but be fure to butter the plate very well that it goes in.
In cafe it is fired below meat, pour off
all the fat from it before you fend it to
the table; ftrew fugar over it.

The Poor Knights of Windfor.

Cut fome flices of bread about half
an inch thick; lay them to foak a while
in white wine and fugar; caft two or
three yolks of eggs; take the bread out
of the wine, and dip it amongft the
eggs; have fome frefh butter boiling in
the frying-pan; put in the bread, and
fry them a fine brown; then difh them,
and

and ſtrew ſugar and beat cinnamon over them : you may eat them with wine if you chooſe.

To make ſmall Curd Puddings.

Earn two pints of new milk; lay it on the back of a ſearce until all the whey is run from it; beat it very well in a mortar with eight ounces of freſh butter, till they are all well mixed together; caſt ſix eggs, and keep out three of the whites; beat two ounces of biſcuit; mix the eggs and biſcuit well with the curd; ſeaſon it with ſugar and beat cinnamon to your taſte, and the grate of a lemon; butter ſome tea-cups, and let one of them be larger than the reſt for the middle; put the ſtuff into the tea-cups, and fire them in a ſlow oven; when they are enough, turn them out on the diſh, the large one in the middle, and the ſmall ones round it; cut ſome blanched almonds in ſmall ſtrips, and ſtick them in the tops of the puddings; pour beat-butter, wine, and ſugar, over them.

To

To make a Curd Florentine.

Take two pounds of curds, and break them very well with your hands; blanch and beat a pound of almonds, with a little rofe or orange-flower water ; pick and wafh half a pound of currants; boil fome fpinage ; cut it fmall with a knife, and fweeten it to your tafte ; oil eight ounces of frefh butter ; mix all well together ; make a fine puffed pafte ; lay a thin covering over all the difh ; then put in the ftuff; cover it on the top with a thin pafte neatly cut out or barred over ; put it in a flow oven to bake : when the pafte is enough, the florentine is ready.

To ftew Parfnips.

Boil them tender, and fcrape them clean ; cut them in flices ; take as much fweet cream as be fauce, and thicken it with butter wrought in flour : when the cream and butter is warm enough, put in the parfnips, and keep it toffing on

the

the fire: when the cream boils they are enough; ſtrew a little ſalt on them.

Boil ſome bitroot, and ſcrape off the ſkins; ſlice it down in thin ſlices; beat ſome freſh butter; put a little vinegar in it; throw in the bitroot: toſs them until they are warm, and diſh them.

To ſtew Red Cabbage.

Cut it down as for pickling; put it in a ſtew-pan with ſome red wine and a piece of butter knead in flour; ſeaſon it with a little ſalt and ſpices; keep it ſtirring until the butter is melted; then cover the pan, and let them ſtew a little, but not too ſoft; for they are better to eat a little criſp; put in a little vinegar before you take them off; diſh them, and ſend them up hot.

To ſtew Cucumbers.

Pare ſome large cucumbers, and ſlice them about the thickneſs of half a crown; ſpread them on a clean coarſe cloth to drain the water from them; pare and ſlice ſome large onions round-
ways;

ways; flour the cucumbers, and fry
them and the onions in browned butter;
when you fee them brown, take them
up carefully from that butter; take a
clean pan, and put three or four fpoonfuls of warm water in it; put in a quarter of a pound of frefh butter rolled in
flour; ftir it on the fire until it is melted; mix in a tea-fpoonful of the flour
of muftard; put in the cucumbers, and
feafon it with falt and fpices; cover up
the pan, and let them ftew about a quarter of an hour, foftly fhaking the pan,
and fo difh them.

To drefs Parfnips to eat like Skirrets.

Boil fome large parfnips tender, and
fcrape off the fkins; cut them by the
length, and cut every piece round, a-
bout the fize of a fkirret, and fry them
in butter a fine light brown; take them
out of the butter, and lay them neatly
i na difh; ftrew beat cinnamon and fugar over them before you fend them to
the table.

Celery,

Celery with Cream.

Wafh and clean the celery ; cut it in
pieces about two or three inches long ;
boil them in water until they are tender ; put them through a drainer, and
keep them warm ; take about half a
mutchkin of fweet cream ; roll a bit of
frefh butter about the bulk of a nutmeg
in flour ; keep it ftirring on the fire until it comes a-boil ; have the yolks of
four eggs ready caft ; mix them with a
little cold cream ; then mix in the boiling cream by degrees amongft the eggs,
and put it on the fire again ; keep it
clofe ftirring, but don't let it boil : throw
in the celery, and give it a tofs up ; feafon it with falt and nutmeg to your tafte,
and difh it.

To ftew Celery in Gravy.

Boil and order the celery as in the a-
bove receipt ; brown a piece of butter,
and thicken it with flour ; mix in as
much good gravy amongft it as will
cover the celery, and a little red wine,
and

and falt and fpices to your tafte; when the fauce comes a-boil, throw in the celery, and let it ftew a little, and then difh it.

To have a Difh of Kidney Beans in the Winter.

Gather the kidney-beans while they are young; ftrew a good deal of falt in the bottom of a can; then lay in fome of the beans, and ftrew in fome more dry falt, and fo continue until the can is full: between every row of beans lay a row of falt; as you lay them in, prefs them pretty hard with your hand, but not fo as to bruife them: when the pot is full, tie them clofe up with a bladder and a piece of leather above it: when you are going to ufe them in the winter, take up what quantity you want, and lay them in frefh water, fome hours before you boil them; change the water two or three times to draw the falt out of them; cut them about an inch long; let the water be boiling before you put them in: when they are enough,

drain

drain the water from them, and tofs
them up with fome beat butter. When
you put in the beans, throw in a tea-
fpoonful of pearl-afhes; it makes them
boil both green and tender: it makes
young peafe of a fine green, or any kind
of greens, and does hurt to nothing.
All thefe garden things are very proper
for fupper difhes.

To keep Artichoke Bottoms the whole Year.

Cut the ftalks very clofe to the artichokes: boil them no longer than the
leaves will come out of them; then take
the choke clean from them, and the
ftrings from the outfide of the bottoms,
and lay them on tin-plates when the
oven is near cold; let them ftand a day
or two in it: they won't be dry enough
with this; but you may fet them at a
diftance from the fire, or in the fun to
dry. When the oven is hot at any o-
ther time, you may put them in again,
and fo continue drying them with either
fire, oven, or the fun, until they are as
dry

dry as a board : then put them in paper
bags, and hang them up in a dry place;
when you are going to use them, lay
them in warm water, and let them lie
about four hours, changing the water
often; you muft pour the laft water
boiling hot on them; cut them in flices
after they are foak'd, and boil them tender. If you have plenty of them, they
make a very fine difh, and they are very
good in either fricafee or ragoo fauces,
or any fine foups.

*The beft way of keeping green Goofeberries
for Tarts.*

Gather them before they are come to
their full fize; cut off the tops and tails
with fciffars; take wide-mouth'd bottles; be fure they are very clean and
dry; fill them up with the berries, and
cork them; put them into an oven not
fo hot as to break the bottles; let them
ftand until they turn white, and pretty
well fallen: when they are enough,
take them out of the oven; take out the
corks, and tie a muflin rag on the top
of

of the bottles ; then turn the bottles into deep jugs that will hold them ; let
them ftand that way until the whole
juice is run from them, (it is the juice
that fpoils them). When they are very
well drained from their juice, turn back
the bottles ; take one of the bottles and
fill up the reft with : leave as much room
as to cover them with fheep's tallow :
melt it, and let it be as cold as it will
pour on the berries : let them be about
an inch covered with the tallow : then
cork them hard up : dip the corks and
the rings of the bottles amongft melted
bees wax, and tie leather above them.
You may fend them to the Indies, if
you pleafe.

To make white Cuftards.

Take a mutchkin of new milk ; put
it on the fire ; when it comes a-boil,
ftir in as much ground rice as will make
it like thick pottage ; have ready the
whites of three eggs ; caft and mix them
with the milk and rice off the fire ; put
it on the fire again for a little, ftirring
it

it all the time ; but take care that it
does not boil ; fweeten it to your tafte
with fine fugar; wet fome tea-cups with
water, and fill them with the cuftards :
when they are cold they will turn out
on the difh.   Caft the yolks ; mix them
with fome boiling milk ; feafon it with
cinnamon, fugar, and a little wine;
when cold pour it on the cuftards.

To make German Puffs.

Take five eggs ; keep out one of the
yolks; take five fpoonfuls of flour ; beat
them well together with fugar to your
tafte, the fcrape of a nutmeg, and a very
little beat ginger ; mix in a mutchkin
of fweet cream and two ounces of oil'd
butter; caft them all together; butter
the pans, and put them in a quick
oven to fire.   The pan muft be only
half full.

To make Apple Puffs.

Stove the apples, and mafh them very
well ; fweeten them to your tafte ; mix
in a little marmalade or cinnamon with
them ;

them ; make puff'd pafte ; lay a faucer of a midling fize on the pafte, and cut quite round by it ; let the apples be quite cold ; lay a fpoonful of them in the middle of the pafte ; then double the pafte together ; wet it a little in the infide to make it ftick, together; mark it neatly with a knife, or plait it with your fingers round the edges. You may fire them in the oven, or fry them in a frying-pan: they are beft done in the oven.

You may make puffs of any preferved fruit or green goofeberries ftov'd and mafh'd like the apples ; you may make puffs of any good thing you pleafe, fuch as an almond pudding: if you have any left over filling your difh, make one quite round, or in the fhape of a ftar, for the middle, and lay the femicircles round it. If they are rightly made up, they are a very pretty difh.

To make Short Bread.

Take a peck of flour, and four pounds
of

of butter Englifh, or three pounds Scots
weight ; put the butter on to come a-
boil; make a hole in the flour, and pour
the boiling butter in it ; work the flour
and butter a little while together ; pour
in a mutchkin of good yeft amongft the
pafte; work it together, but not too
much ; divide the pafte, and roll it out
oval ; then cut it through the middle,
and plait it at the ends; keep out a little
of the flour to work out the bread; flour
gray paper, and fire the bread on it : if
you make it fweet, allow a pound of fugar to the peck of flour at leaft; if you
want it very rich, put in citron, orange-
peel, and almonds, and ftrew white
carvy on the top ; be fure to mix the
fugar and fruit with the flour before
you wet it ; remember to prick it well
on the top..

To make a rich Bun.

To half a peck of flour ftone and
cut two pounds of raifins, clean two
pounds of currants, take fix ounces of
orange-peel, the fame weight of citron,
                                            and

and as many almonds blanch'd and cut;
mix all thefe together; take a drachm
of cloves, a large nutmeg, half an
ounce of Jamaica pepper, and half an
ounce of ginger; beat them all well together; ftrew them on the fruit, and
mix them very well; make a hole in the
flour; break in a pound of butter Scots
weight in it; pour warm water on the
butter to foften it a little; then work
the flour and it together; fpread the
pafte, and pour on half a mutchkin of
good yeft, and work it up very well,
until the pafte is very light and fmooth;
cut off about the third part of the pafte
for the.fheet; fpread out the reft of the
pafte on the table; put the fruit on it;
pour about a gill of yeft over the fruit,
and work the fruit and pafte very well
together, and make it up round; roll
out the fheet round; lay the bun on the
middle, and gather the fheet round it;
roll it out to the thicknefs you would
have it; run a fork through it in different parts down to the bottom, and prick
it on the top; flour double gray paper
and

and lay the bun on it, and give it a cut
round the fide ; put a binder of double
paper round it to keep it from running
too thin in the oven. The oven muſt
neither be too hot nor too cold.

To make a Fourthpart Plumb-cake.

Clean and pick two pounds and a half
of currants, three quarters of a pound
of citron, as much orange-peel, half a
pound of almonds; blanch and cut them
all into pieces, not too ſmall; take a
fourthpart of flour, and break an Eng-
liſh pound of freſh butter in it, the ſame
way as you do the paſte for the bun ;
give it half a mutchkin of good yeſt ;
the paſte muſt be very light and ſmooth
wrought ; cut off a piece for the ſheet ;
take half an ounce of ginger, half an
ounce of corriander feed, a few cloves,
and about a quarter of an ounce of Jamaica pepper ; all theſe muſt be finely
beat, and about a quarter of an ounce
of caraway feeds; mix all theſe together,
and feafon the fruit with them, and
pour a dram over the fruit. The fruit
and

and pafte is wrought entirely in the fame
way as in the bun, and made up in the
fame manner.

To make a Seed-cake.

Dry a pound of flour before the fire,
or in the oven; beat and fearce a pound
of fugar; weigh a pound of eggs; whifk
the eggs and fugar together until it is
very thick and white; have half a pound
of frefh butter ready; caft it to a cream
with your hand ; when the eggs and
fugar are caft, feafon them with beat ginger, cinnamon, and a few caraway feeds;
put in the butter, and caft it with a
timber fpatala ; have ready cut half a
pound of citron, and as much orange-
peel, and six ounces of almonds blanch'd;
cut the orange -peel in narrow ftrips a-
bout an inch long ; cut the citron in
broad pieces; cut the almonds in two
long ways; break the knots of the flour,
and ftir it in the fugar and eggs ; when
it is well mixed, put in the fruit, and
mix all well together, but do not caft it
much after the flour goes in ; butter
the

the frame or hoop, and fire it in the oven. You may ftrew white caraways on the top, if you choofe.

A Diet-loaf.

Take a pound of fugar beat and fifted : caft a pound of eggs with it, until it is very thick and white ; then put in the feafoning ; beat cinnamon, ginger, fome caraway feeds, and a pound of dried flour : fome choofe it with a little butter, as you have in the feed-cake ; but it is rather lighter without it ; butter the frame, and fire it. You may ftrew caraway on the top of it, if you choofe.

A Currant-cake.

Take a pound of frefh butter : caft it with your hand to a cream ; caft a pound of eggs and a pound of fugar in the fame way as in the above receipt ; when the butter, eggs, and fugar, are well caft, mix them all together, and give them a caft : then mix in a pound of dried flour ; caft them all very well, until the flour is quite fmooth ; then mix in

a

a pound of currants pick'd and clean'd, and some caraway feeds; butter a frame, and put it in the oven.

To make fine Gingerbread.

Take two pounds and a half of flour; mix an ounce of beat ginger with it, and half a pound of brown fugar; cut three quarters of a pound of orange-peel and citron not too fmall; mix all thefe together; take a mutchkin and a half of good treacle, and melt it on the fire; beat five eggs; wet the flour with the treacle and eggs; weigh half a pound of frefh butter, Scots weight; melt it and pour it in amongft your other materials; cast them all well together; butter a frame, and put it in the oven. This gingerbread won't fire without frames. If it rifes in blifters when it is in the oven, run a fork through it. It makes very fine plain bread without the fruit, with a few caraway feeds. All thefe cakes muft be fired in an oven neither too hot nor too cold. The way to know when the cakes are fired enough,

is to run a clean knife down the middle
of them; if the knife comes out dry,
they are enough; if the least of it sticks
to the knife, put it into the oven again.

To make common Bifcuit.

Caft a pound of eggs with a pound of
fugar pounded and fifted; dry a pound
of flour; when the eggs and fugar are
very thick and well caft, ftir in the
pound of dried flour and fome caraway
feeds; drop them on paper, and glaze
them on the top with fugar.

To make the fame Bifcuit proper for beating to put in fine Puddings.

Keep out a little of the flour and all
the feeds; and after they are fired fit
for eating, put them in a cold oven to
dry.

To make Savoy Bifcuit.

Caft fix eggs, and a pound of fugar
pounded and fifted, until they are very
thick and white; mix in three quarters
of a pound of fine flour; drop them
oval

190 COOKERY and PASTRY.

oval on paper ; glaze them on the top
with fugar, and fend them to the oven.

To make Spunge Bifcuit.

Caft nine eggs until they frothe ;
pound and fift a pound of fine fugar ;
then beat it up with the eggs till it is
quite fmooth ; mix in three quarters of
a pound of flour and the grate of a lemon or two ; have the bifcuit frames
well buttered with frefh butter ; fill
them a little more than half full, and
put them in the oven.

To make common Almond Bifcuit.

Blanch a pound of fweet almonds ;
beat them up by degrees with the white
of an egg, until they fpread fmooth between your finger and thumb ; have
ready pounded and fifted two pounds
of fine fugar ; pound and fift two hard
bakes ; caft the whites of thirteen eggs;
beat the almonds and eggs together until they are very light ; mix in the fugar by degrees, ftill continuing beating;
mix the bakes with half a pound of
flour ;

flour; then mix all together; drop them oval on paper, and glaze them on the top with fugar, and put them in the oven.

To make Ratafia Drops.

Blanch and beat a pound of almonds, the one half bitter and the other fweet; beat them with the white of an egg as in the former receipt; have ready three more whites of eggs; caft and mix them very well with the pounded almonds; then mix in by degrees a pound of fine fugar pounded and fifted; mix all well together; then drop them off the point of a knife on common white paper, a-bout the bignefs of a fmall coat-button; put them into a cool oven, and fire them.

To make Squirt, Fruit, and Shaving Bifcuit.

Blanch and beat two pounds of fweet almonds, with two whites of eggs, till they are very fmooth; pound and fift two pounds of fine fugar; have the whites of five eggs caft; mix the eggs and

and almonds very well together in the mortar with the end of the peſtle till they are quite white; then put in the ſugar by degrees, ſtirring them conſtantly until they are thoroughly mixed; then put the ſtuff into a clean pan, and ſet it on a ſlow fire, keeping it ſtirring conſtantly until it becomes white and thin. Before you ſet it on the fire, have ſome white wafers ready; whenever the ſtuff comes off the fire, take about the third part of it, and ſpread it on the wafers; make it very ſmooth, and about the thickneſs of a common biſcuit; ſcore it with a knife about an inch broad, and the length of the wafer; but take care not to cut the wafer until after they are fired; then cut the wafer through with a penknife. After the ſhaving biſcuit is dropt, the pan muſt be put on again until it becomes thin; then take the half of what is left in the pan and put it in a bowl; mix four ounces of orange-peel and citron in it cut ſmall; drop them oval on the papers, and ſquirt the remaining part through a mould. You may turn

them

them round, or into any fhape you pleafe. All bifcuit, except ratafia drops, do beft to be dropt on gray paper. Thefe fine bifcuits take very little firing.

CHAP. V.

PRESERVES, PICKLES, &c.

To clarify Sugar.

To every pound of fugar allow half a mutchkin of water, the white of an egg to every two pounds; caft the eggs very well, and put them amongft the water break the fugar, and pour the water and the whites of the eggs upon it; let it ftand to foften a little before you put it on the fire; ftir it on the fire until the fugar is quite diffolved : when the fugar comes a-boil, and the fcum rifes very well, pour in a little cold water, and let it boil a little longer; it makes the fcum rife the better : take the pan off the fire, and let it fettle a little; then fcum it, and lay the fcum on a hair-fearce. All the

the fyrup will run from it, fo that you
will lofe nothing but the drofs; put the
fyrup again on the fire; pour a little
water on it when it comes a-boil: this
brings up a fecond fcum; let it boil a
little: then fet off the pan again; let it
fettle a little, and take off the fcum, and
then the fyrup is for ufe.

To make Smooth Marmalade.

Weigh the oranges; take the fame
weight of fugar as of oranges; wipe all
the oranges with a wet cloth, and grate
them: cut the oranges long ways in
quarters: ftrip off the fkins; fcrape all
the pulp off the inner fkins with a knife,
and pick all the feeds clean from them:
then put on the fkins to boil, until they
are fo tender that they will beat to a
mafh. When you take the fkins off the
fire, fqueeze the water out of them, and
fcrape all the ftrings out of them: clarify the fugar; then take the pounded
fkins, and mix by degrees with the fyrup with a fpoon, juft as if you were
breaking ftarch: when it is all well
mix'd.

mix'd, put it into the pan, and let it boil until the fugar is incorporated with it; then put in the pulp, let it boil until it is all of an equal thicknefs. You will know when it is enough, by its turning heavier in ftirring, and of a finer colour: whenever it begins to fpark it is enough; pound the grate in a mortar; take off the marmalade, and ftir in the grate carefully; when it is all in, put on the pan again, and let it boil until it is all thoroughly mixed. You may keep out fome of the grate, unlefs you choofe it very bitter. If you fave any of the grate, dry it, and keep it for feafonings.

To make Chip Marmalade.

Weigh the oranges, and take equal weight of fugar; clean and grate the oranges, as in the former receipt; cut them crofs, and fqueeze them through a fearce; boil the fkins tender, fo that the head of a pin will pierce them: when you take them off the fire, fqueeze the water out of them, and fcrape all the
ftrings

strings from them; cut them into very
thin chips, and let them boil until they
are tranfparent. As foon as the oranges
are grated, pour fome boiling water on
them, and cover them up until you are
ready to ufe them: when the chips are
quite trafparent, put in the juice, and
ftrain the water through a fearce from
the gratings in amongft the marmalade,
and let all boil together until the juice
jellies, which you will know by letting
a little of it cool in a faucer.

It may be expected, that I might have
given many more different receipts for
making marmalade; but I may venture
to fay, that there is not many ways of
making it; and I have tried, and found
by experience, that thefe two receipts
are the beft.

To preferve whole Oranges.

Lay the oranges into falt and water
for two days; take them out of that,
and wafh them clean with frefh water;
lay frefh water on them, and let them
ly a day in it, to take the falt out of
them;

them ; then grate or ridge them ; put
them on in a clofe copper-pot with
plenty of water about them ; let them
boil until they are fo tender that the
head of a pin will eafily pierce them ;
take them out of the water while they
are warm ; cut a round piece out of the
top, and take out the pulp and the
feeds with the fhank of a tea-fpoon ;
clarify as much fugar as will cover and
boil the oranges ; be fure not to fcrimp
them of fyrup, nor put them into too
fmall a pan. In this fyrup, you muft
allow half a gill more water to the
pound of fugar than the common fyrup,
otherwife the fugar would candy before
it would penetrate into the orange, as
they take a long time to boil ; keep
them gently down amongft the fyrup
as they are boiling ; let them boil about
three quarters of an hour ; then take
off the pan, and let them ftand until they
are almoft cold ; put them on the fire
again, and let them boil until they are
of a fine colour, and quite tranfparent ;
put every orange into a fmall pot ; fill
up

up the orange with fyrup, and put on
the tops ; put as much fyrup into each
pot as will cover the orange. If you
have not enough of fyrup left, you muft
make more, as the oranges fpoil when
they are not well covered with it.

To preferve Orange-fkins.

Lay them in falt and water as you
do the whole oranges ; grate them, and
cut them through the middle ; fqueeze
out the juice, and pick out all the inner fkins ; boil them until they are fo
tender that the head of a pin will eafily
pierce them ; be fure you fcrape all the
ftrings from them ; cafe the fkins in one
another, and put them into a pot that
will hold them eafily ; clarify as much
fugar as will cover them, and pour the
fyrup on the fkins when it is quite cold.
It muft be a wide-mouth'd pot that will
let in a faucer ; put a little weight on the
faucer to hold down the fkins amongft
the fyrup ; let them ftand for four or
five days; by that time the fyrup will
become as thin as water. You muft take
it

it off, and boil it up with more fugar, until the fyrup is of a proper thicknefs; let it cool, and pour it on the fkins a-gain ; let them ftand for eight or ten days, and the fyrup will be thin again, though not fo thin as before; take it off, and add more fugar to it; when it boils, fcum it very clean ; put in the fkins a-mongft it, and let them boil until they are quite tranfparent ; then cafe them one within another, and lay them in the pot, and pour the fyrup over them ; be fure to have as much as will cover them, and lay them by for ufe. Three or four of the fkins turned down, with a flice of preferved oranges between each of them, make a very pretty affet.

Preferved fliced Oranges.

Grate the oranges ; cut them crofs in thin flices ; pick the feeds carefully out with a bodkin, but take care not to break the pulp ; lay them in a flat bot-tom'd jar, one flice above another ; cla-rify as much fugar as will cover them ; and when the fyrup is cold, pour it
over

over them; put a weight on them to
keep them down amongſt the ſyrup; let
them ſtand two or three days ; by that
time the ſyrup will be very thin ; then
turn out the ſlices on a hair-ſearce to
drain all the liquor from them ; add as
much ſugar to the liquor as make it into a good ſyrup ; be ſure to ſcum it always when it boils ; put back the ſlices
into the pot, and when the ſyrup is cold,
pour it on them ; let them ſtand eight
or ten days. You muſt repeat this a
third time in the ſame manner : it is a
long time before the ſyrup penetrates
into the heart of the raw oranges ; let
them ſtand for eight days longer ; then
pour off the ſyrup, and boil it up with
ſome more ſugar ; take off the ſcum ;
then put in the ſlices, and give them a
hearty boil. When you put the ſlices in
the pan, cover them with clean white
paper. When the oranges have got two
or three hearty boils, take them off the
fire, and let them ſtand until they are
almoſt cold, and don't take the paper
off them ; then put the ſlices neatly up,
and

and pour the fyrup over them; be fure you have always fyrup to cover them. This is a very good and a very pretty preferve.

To preferve Orange Grate.

Boil the grated fkins tender; pound them as for fmooth marmalade; take one pound of fugar to a pound of the pounded fkins; clarify the fugar; and boil the fkins amongft the fyrup, juft as you do the fmooth marmalade; when they are thoroughly boiled, ftir in as much of the grate as will make them like thick pottage; let it get a boil or two to mix it well; then pot it up for ufe. This is better for orange puddings, or any thing that is to be feafoned with o-ranges, than even frefh oranges or mar-malade. You fhould dry the orange-grate as you gather it; for although it is dry, it will make this conferve very well: likewife keep all the parings of your lemons; pare them thin, and lay them by for ufe. When they are well
dried

dried, they will ferve for feafoning any thing that lemon-peel fhould go into.

Orange Chips.

Take the thin pairings of oranges, and boil them in water until they are tender; clarify as much fugar as will cover them, and pour it on them when cold. You may let them lie for two or three days; then pour it off, and boil it up again: and when cold pour it over the fkins. Do this three or four times, until the chips are tranfparent; then take them out of the fyrup, and cut them into pieces of what length you choofe; fpread them on plates with the white fides upmoft, until the fyrup is dried from them; then candy them as you do the orange-peel.

To make Orange-peel.

Lay the orange fkins in falt and water three or four days; then put them on with cold water, and let them boil until they are tender; fcrape out all the pulp and ftrings; make and clarify as
much

much good rich fyrup as will cover
them; cafe the fkins one within another, and put them into a ftone jar;
when the fyrup is cold, pour it over
them, and let them ftand until the fyrup is thin about them; then pour it
off them, and add more fugar to it;
boil it up to a good fyrup, and when it
is cold, pour it on the fkins again, and
let it lie on them until the are quite
tranfparent; take the fkins out of that
fyrup; boil up fome fugar to a candy
height; then put in the fkins, keeping
them ftirring from the pan until they
begin to candy; take them up and
fpread them on fieves until they are
cold.

To candy Angelica.

Take the angelica in the month of
May, while it is tender; cut away the
leaves; cut the ftalks in pieces about a
quarter long; lay them in cold water
as you cut them; fet them on the fire
in a panful of water; let them boil
tender and green; then take them out
and

and peel them; and as they are peeled, throw them into a panful of warm water. For every pound of angelica take a pound and a quarter of double-refin'd sugar; take the half of the sugar, and make it into a ſtrong ſyrup; lay the angelica in the ſyrup for eight or ten days; then take it out of that ſyrup, and put the other half of the ſugar into the ſyrup; clarify, ſcum, and boil it candy height; tie up the angelica to what ſhape you chooſe; then put it into the ſugar; let it boil dry amongſt the ſugar, keeping the pan always ſhaking. When it is enough lay it on ſieves to dry.

To candy Flowers.

Take any kind of flowers you think pretty; if the ſtalks are very long, cut off ſome of them; clarify and boil a pound of fine ſugar till near candy height; when the ſugar begins to grow ſtiff, and ſomething cool, dip the flowers into it; take them out immediately, and lay them one by one on a ſieve; dry them in a ſtove.

To

To make Red-currant Jelly.

Take the largeſt berries you can get; ſtrip them off the ſtalks; do not put in green ones, nor the red hard berries that are at the end of the ſtalks, for they have neither juice nor taſte. After the berries are ſtript, weigh them, and take the ſame weight of ſingle-refined ſugar; clarify the ſugar, and let it boil to candy-height, which you will know by the ſugar boiling thick like pottage; take up ſome of the ſyrup with a ſpoon, and if it hangs in broad flakes when you pour it out, it is enough; then throw in the whole berries into the ſyrup, and let them boil very faſt for ten or eleven minutes at the longeſt; then lay a hair-ſearce on a deep can; pour it into the ſearce, and all the jelly will run through; ſtir the berries gently up with a ſpoon; but take care you do not bruiſe any of them, for by ſo doing the whole will run through; there will be nothing left in the ſearce but the ſkins and ſeeds. While the jelly is running through, cauſe

K   clean

clean the pan it was boiled in, and turn
back the jelly into it : warm it on the
fire, but take care it do not boil ; fo pot
it up. This manner of making jelly
preferves more of the pure juice of the
fruit than by ftraining them through a
cloth, which fpoils the flavour and colour ; and it neither candies nor runs,
which in the common way of making
it is apt to do.

White-currant Jelly.

Bruife the berries with the back of a
fpoon, and run the juice through a jelly
bag. To every mutchkin of juice take
a pound of double-refined fugar ; clarify
and boil it to a candy-height ; then put
in the juice, and let it boil about ten
minutes ; take off all the fcum that
comes from the juice ; put it through a
fearce, and then put it up in pots.

Black-currant Jelly.

To three pints of black currants take
one pint of red ; ftrip them from the
ftalk; put them with half a mutchkin
of

of water into a can, and tie them clofe
up with fome folds of paper ; then put
the can into a pot of water, and let it
boil about twelve hours ; but take care
none of the water goes into 'the can ;
and as the water boils down, you may
add fome more to it ; turn the berries
into a fearce ; bruife them with the back
of a fpoon on the fide of it ; then gather
all the bruifed berries together, and put
them into a clean bowl ; pour on a
mutchkin of water ; bruife them well
with a fpoon ; turn them into a fearce,
and let them ftand all night ; let the
water that runs through be put amongft
the juice ; by fo doing, you get the
whole ftrength of the berries. This is
much better than ftraining through a
cloth, which both fpoils the tafte and
colour of the fruit. To every mutchkin
of juice take a pound of fugar ; clarify
and boil it to candy-height ; then put
in the juice ; let it boil a quarter of an
hour, taking off the fcum as it rifes,
and then pot it up.

To preserve whole Currants.

Pick all the berries off the ftalks, or clip them off with a pair of fciffars, which is neater; likewife the black tops of the berries ; but take care you do not break the berries ; take equal weight of fingle-refined fugar and currants ; keep out a little of the fugar, which pound and fearce, and clarify the reft, and boil it candy-height; take the half of the berries, and throw them into the fyrup; let them boil eight minutes, as you do the jelly ; run them through the fearce in the fame way. When it is all through the fearce, put it into the pan ; and whenever it comes to boil, put in the whole berries, after ftrewing them over with the pounded fugar, and let the whole boil together five minutes ; then take them off, and pot them up. White currants may be done in the fame way; only be fure you ufe double-refin'd fugar. This is a pretty preferve in glaffes or fine tarts. If you have a mind to do a few of them upon ftalks, you muft make a

fmall

fmall hole in the fide with the point of a pin, and pick out all the feeds ; ftrew a little pounded fugar on the bottom of a plate, and lay every ftalk feparate; ftrew fome of the pounded fugar over them ; put them in at the fame time with the whole berries: when they are done, you can eafily feparate the berries on the ftalks from the whole ones ; put them into glaffes, and fill them up with the jelly, and let the ends of the ftalks be uppermoft in the glaffes.

An excellent way of doing Currants for prefent ufe.

Caft the whites of two or three eggs, until they drop from the fpoon like wa-ter ; take the largeft and beft red cur-rants you can get ; keep them on the ftalks ; have fome double-refined fugar pounded and fifted ; take every ftalk of the berries by itfelf; dip them in the eggs as above ; and while they are wet, roll them gently in the fugar ; lay them fo as not to touch each other on a fheet of clean white paper before the fire to
dry ;

dry; but take care you don't burn them; put them on a china plate, and fo fend them to table. If there are any green berries at the end of the ftalk, be fure to pick them off.

To preferve Rafberries whole.

Take the beft you can get; and to every pound of them take a pound and a half of fingle-refined fugar; clarify and boil it candy-high; keep a little of the fugar out to pound and fift; when the fugar is ready, put in the rafps, and let them boil as quick as poffible; ftrew the pounded fugar over them as they boil; when the fugar boils over them, take them off the fire, and let them ftand until they are almoft cold. To every pound of rafps put half a mutch-kin of currant juice, which put in a-mongft them; then put the whole on to boil, till the fyrup hangs in flakes from the fpoon; keep fcumming as they rife; then take it off, and put it in pots or glaffes.

Straw—

Strawberries are preserved in the same manner.

To make Rasberry Jam.

Pick and clean the berries well. To every pound of berries take half a mutchkin of the juice of currants, and a pound and a half of lump sugar; pound it, and put it into a pan, a row of fruit and a row of sugar alternately; let the whole stand in the pan some time before you put them on the fire, to soften the sugar; boil them on a quick fire, and when they fall to the bottom they are enough.

To preserve Green Gooseberries.

Take the largest and greenest gaskens you can get; cut off the black tops, and leave the tails; slit them down the side with a pin, but not too long; put in a bowl as much water as will cover them; beat a good piece of alum; put it into the water to dissolve. As you cut and open the berries, throw them into the water until they are all done; then

then put them on the fire to fcald, but
take care they don't boil; take them
out very carefully with a fkimmer, and
fpread them on the back of a fcarce to
drain the water from them. You muft
not lay one above another, for bruifing
them. Weigh the berries before you do
any thing to them; and to every pound
of berries take two pounds of double-
refin'd fugar; clarify the fugar. You
may lay by near one half of the fyrup,
and the other half put in a pan until it
boil; then put in a few of the berries
carefully; let them boil just one minute:
take them up carefully, and put them
into fmall pots; repeat boiling the reft
in the fame manner and time until they
are all done; put the fyrup through a
fcarce, to keep out the feeds; pour it
hot upon the berries, and lay fome light
thing over them to keep them down a-
mongft the fyrup; let them ftand five
days; then drain all the fyrup from
them, which will be very thin; add to
it a part of that kept out; let it come to
boil; throw in the berries, and give
them,

them another minute's boiling as at firft,
and lay them by in the fame manner as
before; let them ftand ten days; add
new fyrup to the old, and give them the
fame boiling as before; put them up
and let them ftand other eight or ten
days. If they are not green enough,
give them another boil in the fame way;
be fure every time you take off the fyrup
to run it through a fearce, which takes
out the feeds better than picking them
out with a pin, and much eafier. When
they are fo done, and quite cold, cover
them up clofe with paper.

To preferve Red Goofeberries.

Take the beft Mogul berries; take off
the black tops, and leave the ftalks, as
in the preceding receipt; take equal
weight of berries and fingle refined fugar; clarify the fugar; make a very
fmall flit in the berries with a pin on
the fide, which lets the fugar go through
them. When the fyrup is ready, put
in the berries, and let them boil till the
fugar is quite into the heart of them,

and

and become tranfparent; then take
them up with a fkimmer; put them
into pots, and run the fyrup through a
fearce, to keep out the feeds; put the
fyrup into a pan again, and let it boil
until it ropes from the fpoon; then
pour it on the berries; don't let the berries boil on too ftrong a fire. You may
put them into glaffes, as they look very
fine.

To make Goofeberry Jam.

Take the fame weight of powder-fu-
gar as of berries; put in the berries,
ftrewing the fugar over them as you
put them in; pour half a mutchkin of
water over them; put them on a flow
fire; let them boil flowly a little time;
fkim them as clean as you can; then
put a quicker fire to them; let them boil
till they are very clear, and will jelly.
So pot them up.

To make Goofeberry Jelly.

Fill a ftone jar with ripe goofeberries; cover it clofe up with paper; put
it

it in a pot of water; let them boil until
they are quite tender, juft as you do
black currants; then put them through
a fearce. To every mutchkin of juice
take a pound of fingle-refin'd fugar;
clarify it, and boil it candy-high; then
put in the juice, and let it boil till it
jellies, which you will eafily know by
letting a little of it cool on a faucer;
take off any fcum that rifes from the
fruit before you pot it up.

To preferve Cherries.

Cut off part of each ftalk. To every
pound of cherries take a pound of
fingle refin'd fugar; clarify and boil it
candy-high: put in the cherries, and
let them boil as quick as you can, until
the fyrup entirely covers them: when
they have boiled a little time, fcum
them, and let them ftand till next day.
To very two pounds of cherries take a
mutchkin of the juice of red currants,
and allow a pound of fugar to the
mutchkin of juice; pour off the fyrup
from the cherries, and put it on the
fire

fire with the currant-juice ; let it boil ;
fcum it, and then put in the cherries ;
let all boil together for two or three
minutes ; and when they are almoft
cold, place them in pots or glaffes, and
pour the fyrup over them.——Morella
cherries are better than the common
ones ; but as the feafon of them is late,
the currants are commonly over before
they are ripe ; in that cafe, you muft
take currant-jelly.

To preferve Cherries with Stalks and Leaves.

Take the largeft May-duke cherries ;
gather them carefully with the ftalks,
and fome of the leaves on them ; take
fome ftrong vinegar, and beat a little
alum in it ; put it on the fire, and let it
boil ; then dip in the ftalks and leaves,
and give them a little boil in the vinegar, (but take care you don't let the
cherries touch the vinegar) ; then lay
them on a fearce to dry ; clarify two
pounds of double refin'd fugar. While
the fyrup is boiling hot, dip the cherries,
ftalks,

ftalks, and leaves in it. When they are
fcalding hot, take them out again, and
lay them on the fearce; then boil up
the fyrup candy-high; dip the cherries
into it again; then lay them again on
the fearce; dry them in the fun, or in
a drying ftove; turn them frequently
whilft on the fearce.

To preferve Apricots.

Take the largeft and beft you can
get, juft ripe, and no more; open them
at the crefs with a knife, and thruft out
the ftone with a bodkin; pare them as
thin as you can. To every pound of
apricots take a pound and a half of
fine fugar. As you pare then, ftrew
fome pounded fugar on them; clarify
the remainder of the fugar; put the a-
pricots in the fyrup, and let them lie
till the fyrup is almoft cold; then put
them on a flow fire, and let them fimmer on the fire a little; cover them with
white paper; fet them off the fire, and
let them ftand until they are almoft cold;
then put them on again, and bring them

to

to a fimmer ; repeat this three or four
times, letting them be almoft cold before you put them on; by this time the
fugar will be well incorporate with
them ; then put on, and bring them to
the boil ; let them boil until they are
quite tranfparent. If you choofe you
may blanch the kernels, and put them
in amongft them at the laft boiling.
So pot them up.

To make Apricot Jam.

Stone and pare the apricots ; take
equal weight of fugar and fruit; clarify
the fugar and boil it candy-height ; put
in the apricots, and let them boil very
thick, until they are well broke. You
may bruife them with a fpoon as they
boil : you may boil a little white currant jelly with them, for they are much
the better of it ; blanch the kernels, and
mix with them juft before you take them
off. This makes very fine tarts.

To preferve Green Gauge Plumbs.

Pluck the plumbs when full grown,
with

with the ftack at each, and a leaf, if you
can ; let them lie in cold water twenty-
four hours ; take them out of that water ; put two or three green-kail blades
in the bottom of a clean brafs-pan ; put
in the fruit, with as much water as will
wholly cover them; ftrew a little pounded alum amongft them ; put them on a
clear fire; and when they rife to the top,
take them out, and put them in a bowl
with a little warm water about them ;
clean the pan again; put in a frefh
green-kail blade in the pan ; put as
much boiling water on them as will
cover them, with a little more pounded
alum ; cover them with a cloth ; let
them ftand a quarter of an hour ; take
them out of the water ; weigh them,
and take equal weight of double-refin'd
fugar ; pound the fugar ; clean the pan
again ; put in the fruit, and ftrew the
pounded fugar alongft them, and a
little water ; fet it on a clear fire, and
let it fimmer and boil flowly, until the
fruit is green and tranfparent ; put the
fruit in pots ; boil the fyrup a little
longer ;

longer; and when it is cold, pour it on the fruit; let them ftand two or three days; then pour off the fyrup; boil it up with more fugar to a ftrong fmooth fyrup: when it is cold, pour it on the fruit, and clofe them up; and as the fkin will fhrivel down, you muft take it gently off.

To preferve Magnum Plumbs.

Take the plumbs before they are too ripe, and give them a flit on the hollow fide with a pen-knife, and prick them with a pin; take fcalding hot water, and put a little fugar in it; put in the plumbs; cover them clofe up, and fet them on a flow fire to fimmer; take them off, and let them ftand a little; put them on the fire again to fimmer, but take care they do not break; clarify as much fugar as will cover the plumbs, and boil it to candy-height: when the plumbs are pretty tender, take them out of that liquor, and put them amongft the fyrup when it is almoft cold, till they are very tranfparent; fkim

fkim them, and take them off; let them ftand about two hours; then fet them on, and give them another boil; put them in pots or glaffes; boil up the fyrup very thick; and when it is cold pour it over the plumbs.

To keep common Plumbs for Tarts.

Put the plumbs into a narrow-mouth'd ftone-jar. To every twelve pounds of plumbs take feven pounds of raw fugar, and ftrew it in amongft the plumbs as you put them in the jar; tie up the mouth of the pot very clofe with feveral folds of paper; put them into a flow oven and let them ftand until the fugar has quite penetrated them, and then they are enough.

To preferve Peaches.

Put the peaches into boil'd water, but don't let them boil; take them out, and put them into cold water; then lay them between two cloths to dry. To every dozen of peaches clarify a pound of fugar; when you take the peaches

out

out the cloth, prick them with a pin ;
put them into a clofe-mouth'd jar ; and
when the fyrup is cold, pour it over
them, and fill up the jar with brandy ;
put a wet bladder on the mouth of the
jar ; and tie leather above it.

To preferve Pears.

Take the beft preferving pears new
pluck'd ; make a fmall hole at the black
end with a fmall ivory bodkin, and pick
out the feeds ; pare them very thin ;
weigh them, and take equal weight of
fine fugar ; take half a mutchkin of the
water that boil'd the pears to each pound
of fugar ; clarify it, and put in the
pears ; let them boil until they are foft.
When you put the pears into pots, boil
up the fyrup again, and pour it over
them : when it is quite cold, put a clove
into every pear where the eye was cut
out ; cover them with the jelly of apples
and fo pot them up.

To preferve Pears red.

Take the largeft pound-pears when
full

full ripe; pare them, and put them into as much water as will cover them;
pound a drop or two of cochineal, and
put it into the water; let them boil till
they are tender; keep them close covered while the fyrup is making; weigh
them, and take equal weight of fugar;
clarify it; then put in the pears; fqueeze
the juice of a lemon amongft the fyrup,
and cut the thin pairing of the lemon as
fmall as you can, and put in it: let
them boil until they are red and tranf--
parent; then put them into pots; and
when the fyrup is cold, pour it over
them; cover them with the jelly of red
goofeberries; pick out the feeds, as in
the preceding receipt, and put a clove
into every pear.

To make Apple Jelly.

Pare a dozen of good tart apples;
take a pint of water; cut the apples in
very fmall bits, and throw them into
the water as you cut them, to preferve
their colour; let them boil until the
whole fubftance is out of them, and
the

the water half wasted ; then put it into
a hair-fearce ; let them stand until all
the water is drain'd from them. To
every mutchkin of the liquor take a
pound of fine sugar ; cast the white of
an egg or two, and put in amongst the
sugar and liquor ; put them on the fire,
and keep them stirring until the sugar
is melted ; when it boils a while, take
off the scum, and put in the juice of a
lemon or two, as you like it of tartness.
You may boil in a piece of the rhind
along with them ; let it boil until it
jellies, which you will know by putting
a little of it on a saucer to cool ; take all
the scum clean off, and take out the lemon. So pot it up.

Chip and Jelly of Apples.

Prepare the apples in the same way
as in the foregoing receipt for the jelly ;
pare the apples, cut them in slices, and
then cut the slices into long chips (as
you do the chip marmalade); put them
amongst cold water. You may weigh
two pounds of apples before you pare
them.

them. To each chopin of juice allow
two pounds of fine fugar, and a pound
and a half for the two pounds of chips ;
put on all the fugar and juice ; clarify
it with the eggs as you do the jelly; when
the , fyrup is well fcummed, fqueeze in
the juice of three lemons, put in it fome
of the parings of the lemons : drain the
water from the chips, and put them into the fyrup ; they muft boil on a quick
fire ; let them boil until the chips are
quite tranfparent. You muft be fure
that they are very firm apples. The
true leadington anfwers very well, or the
pippins. This is a very pretty preferve,
either in glaffes or fine tarts.

To preferve Apples green.

Take the large coddling, or any other
hard green apple ; they muft be newly
pulled ; cut them in quarters, and cut
out the core ; put them into a brafs pan,
with hard water and a little pounded
alum ; turn the green fide downmoft ;
let them fimmer on a flow fire, but
don't let them boil ; they are enough
when

when you take off the fkin without any
of the fruit adhering to it; and after
they are all peeled, put them on again
amongft the fame water, with two ounces of fugar; keep down the green fide,
and let them fimmer gently for a little
while; put them on and off the fire until they turn green; they muft not be
long at a time on the fire, as they would
become too foft; take out the apples
from the liquor, and lay them on a difh.
To every pound of apples clarify a
pound of fine fugar; when the fyrup is
ready put in the apples, and give them
a quick boil, until they are tranfparent;
take them out of the fyrup, and boil up
the fyrup until it is pretty thick. When
the apples and fyrup are cold, put them
into pots; let them ftand fome days,
and if the fyrup is turned thin, pour it
off the apples, and give them a boil in
it; and when they are cold, put them
into pots, and clofe them up. You may
look at them in a fortnight after; and if
the fyrup is turned thin, boil them up
again as before.

Apples

Apples in Syrup.

Take firm round apples; take out the cores; pare them, and throw them into cold water as you pair them.; clarify as much fine fugar as will cover them; put them into the fyrup, and let them boil on a quick fire until the apples are tranfparent; turn them often in the pan that the fugar may boil over them: place them neatly in a china difh, and pour the fyrup about them; put in the juice of a lemon when the fyrup is clarified. If you have any preferved barberries, you may put in two or three fprigs of them on the top of the apples. This is a very pretty difh for prefent ufe.

To preferve Cucumbers.

Take the greeneft, and not too large, cucumbers you can get, and lay them in a ftrong pickle of falt and water; let them lie four days; take them out of that pickle, and put them in a frefh one as ftrong as the former, and let
them

them lie as long in it as in the firſt; waſh them out of that in clean water, and lay them in plenty of freſh water for twenty-four hours; lay a weight on them to hold them down; make a ſlit in one of the hallows with a pen-knife, and take out all the pulp; lay green blades in the bottom of a pan; then put the cucumbers into the pan; take equal quantity of vinegar and water; more than cover them; put in a good piece of pounded alum and ſaltpetre; ſtrew it in the pan; cover up cloſe with more green blades; put them on the fire, and let them be near the boil; ſet them off the fire, and let them ſtand for an hour or more; ſet them on again, and give them a good quick heat, but not to boil; ſet them off, and let them ſtand as long as before; then put them on the fire again, and give them a quick boil. When that is done, they will turn green; take them up and ſpread them between two cloths, with the cut ſide undermoſt; take thin pairings of lemons, white pepper, ſliced ginger, ſome blades

of

of mace; mix all thefe together, and
ftuff the cucumbers full of them; then
lay them in a flat-bottom'd potting-can
with the cut fide up; have as much
double-refin'd fugar clarified as will cover them. When the fyrup is cold pour
it over them; cover them with a plate
and a weight above it, to hold them
down amongft the fyrup. When the
fyrup is quite thin about them, pour
it off; add more fugar to it, and boil
it up to a good fyrup, and when cold,
pour it over the cucumbers; let it ftand
on them for eight or ten days; then
pour it off, and boil it up again with
more fugar. You muft continue fo doing for every eight or ten days, until
the fugar be quite into the heart of them,
and the cucumbers of a fine green, and
that the fyrup remains thick about them,
then you may pot them up for ufe:
throw in amongft the fyrup, when you
pot them up, fome whole white pepper
and ginger; for they cannot be too much
flavoured of the fpices. You may cut
them into what fhape you pleafe when

you

you fend them to the table alongft with other preferves.

To preferve Melons.

Take the melons before they are quite ripe ; lay them in falt and water two days ; take them out of that pickle, and lay them in cold clean water another day ; green them the fame way as the preferv'd cucumbers : when they are green'd, cut a fmall bit out at one of the ends, and fcoop out all the pulp. Do the fyrup the fame way as for the cucumbers ; let it be quite cold or you put it on the melons ; throw in a good deal of lemon-peel and caffia buds, and fome fliced ginger amongft the fyrup ; and the laft boiling you give the fyrup put in fome of the juice of lemon.

To preferve green Almonds.

Pluck the almonds when not full grown, but fo tender that a pin will pierce through them ; rub them with a clean cloth, and put them into boiling water for three or four minutes, until
the

the outer fkin will rub off with a cloth, have ready fome thick fyrup, and put the almonds in it, and let them boil two minutes; take them out of the fyrup; and boil the fyrup a little longer, and pour it on them; repeat the boiling the fyrup five or fix days, until the fyrup remains thick on them, and that it is penetrated into them. Boil fome rock alum alfo in the water.

All green and white preferves muft be done with double-refin'd fugar, elfe they won't be pretty. Another thing to be minded is, that there is no other pans fit for preferving or pickling but bell-metal or brafs ones, and thefe muft always be clean fcour'd before you ufe them.

To preferve Barberries.

Take the largeft and fineft fprigs of barberries you can get; lay them carefully in a ftone flat-bottom'd pot; clarify as much fine fugar as will cover them: when the fyrup is cold, pour it over

over them ; let it ftand until the fyrup becomes thin; then pour it off them, and add more fugar to it, and boil it to a pretty ftrong fyrup; when cold, pour it over them again, which you muft repeat until the fyrup is incorporated with the berries, and that they are tranfparent, and the fyrup remains thick about them; then pot them up for ufe. When you ufe them, take them up in whole fprigs ; put them into glaffes with the fyrup about them ; they look very pretty. They are a very pretty garnifhing to milk-difhes.

Be fure to put paper dipped in fpirits clofe on all preferves, or in fine oil, which is rather better for keeping them from candying than the fpirits ; take care not to keep them in a damp place, nor in a place too drying.

To make Lemon-fyrup.

Cut the lemons, and fqueeze out the juice; put it into a ftone or china mug; a filver tankard is better, if you have it ; let the juice ftand until it is clear; then

then pour it off from the grounds : let none of that go in. To every mutchkin of juice beat and fift two pounds of double-refin'd fugar, and ftir it in amongft the juice until it is diffolved; clean the tankard, and put the fyrup into it ; put the tankard into a pot of cold water, and let the water boil about it for a quarter of an hour; then take it out of the water, and let it ftand all night ; take off the fcum and when the fyrup is cold, bottle it up. If it is in a mug, you muft tie feveral folds of paper about the mouth of it before you put it into the water.

Syrup of Clove-Julyflower.

Cut all the white ends of them. To every pound of flowers put on a chopin of water, and about a dozen of cloves; put them into a ftone pot, and tie them clofe up with paper, and put it into a pot of cold water; let it boil about them for five or fix hours; take care the water does not boil into the pot ; then take them out, and fqueeze them through a
clean

clean cloth. To every mutchkin of juice take a pound of fine fugar ; put in the white of an egg to clarify it ; fcum it very well as it boils up ; when cold, bottle it up.

Syrup of Violets.

Pick them off the ftalks.   To every pound of violets pour on a mutchkin of boiling water ; cover them up clofe, and let them ftand for twenty-four hours ; then ftrain it. For every mutchkin of juice take two pounds of double-refin'd fugar, pounded and fifted, and put it in by degrees ; and when the fugar is quite diffolved, bottle it up.

Syrup of Pale Rofes.

Fill an earthen pot with rofes ; pour boiling water over them ; cover them up, and let them ftand all next day ; ftrain them through a clean cloth, and add as many frefh rofes to the liquor as you had before ; fet them on the fire, and let them boil until they are ftrong ; then ftrain it. To every mutchkin of
juice

juice take a pound of fine fugar, and
mix it in with the juice ; put in the
white of an egg or two to clarify it ;
then put it on the fire to boil ; it muft
not boil too long ; fcum it very well,
and when cold bottle it up.

Syrup of Maidenhair.

Take half a pound of maidenhair, and
half a pound of liquorice-ftick ; peel off
the fkin, and flice it down ; take an
ounce of tiffilago ; put them all into a
pot that will hold a pint ; fill the pot
with water ; tie it clofe up, and put it
into a pot of cold water ; fet it on the
fire, and let it boil for feven or eight
hours ; then ftrain it through a cloth.
To every mutchkin of juice take a pound
of white fugar-candy ; clarify it with
the white of an egg ; let it boil well ;
fcum it, and when cold bottle it up.

Syrup of Turnip.

Wafh the turnip very clean, and dry
them with a cloth ; grate them down and
ftrain them through a clean cloth. To
every

every mutchkin of juice take a pound
of fugar-candy; clarify it with the
white of an egg; let it boil well; fcum
it, and when cold bottle it up.

Syrup of Nettles.

Take the red nettles in the fpring of
the year; pick and wafh them very clean
through two or three waters; beat them
in a mortar, and fqueeze out the juice;
let it ftand twenty-four hours to fettle;
then pour all the clear juice from the
grounds.   To every mutchkin of juice
take a pound of fugar-candy, and clarify it; boil and fcum it, and when
cold bottle it up.

Conferve of Rofes.

Take the buds of the true fcarlet rofes; clip off all the red part.   To each
pound of rofes beat and fift two pounds
of fine fugar; pound the rofes very well
in a marble mortar; then ftir in the
fugar by degrees, and continue pound-
ing until all the fugar is thoroughly incorporated with the rofes.   If you think
it

it too thin, add more fugar, until they will receive no more.

To make Tablets.

Clarify fome fugar. To every pound of fugar take half an ounce of cinnamon finely pounded and fearced. The fugar muft boil until you can blow it like bladders through the holes of the fkimmer; then mix in the cinnamon; take the pan off the fire, and prefs the fugar againft the fide of the pan with the back of a fpoon, to make it grain; butter a fmooth ftone very well, or a clean pewter difh, or a fheet of clean white paper. You may pin it up at the corners; pour the tablets on either of thefe; let it ftand fome time; then fcore it with a knife in fquares, and when it is quite firm take it off.

You may make ginger-tablet the fame way; and to the pound of fugar take a quarter of an ounce of ginger finely beat and fifted. You may put in more, if you love it ftrong-flavoured of the

the ginger. Superfine cinnamon-tablet muſt be made with the very fineſt of ſugar; and in place of the pounded cinnamon, you muſt put in two tea-ſpoonfuls of the oil of cinnamon. Be ſure to mix the ſeaſoning well amongſt the ſugar before you turn it out of the pan.

To make Barley-ſugar.

Waſh a little barley, and put it on with boiling water; let it boil a little; then turn out that water, and pour more boiling water on it; put on a pennyworth of liquorice-ſtick; let it boil until all the ſtrength is out of it; then pour off the liquor, and let it ſtand to ſettle, and pour all the clear from the grounds; take half a mutchkin of it to the pound of ſugar; clarify it with whites of eggs. It muſt be on a ſoft equal fire: you muſt not ſtir it much on the fire; it muſt be boiled until it crackles. This is a higher degree of boiling the ſugar than blowing. The way to know it, is to dip a ſmall ſtick into clean water; then put it into the boiling ſugar, and try it with your teeth;

teeth; if it ſticks to them like glue, it is not enough. You muſt boil it a little longer, and when you hear it crack between your teeth take it off; have a ſtone ready rubb'd with freſh butter or fine oil; then pour the ſugar on it; you muſt double it together, and cut it as faſt as you can with big ſciſſars; give it a little twiſt as you cut it. If you think the ſugar boils too furiouſly, put a very little bit of freſh butter amongſt it.

To make Glaſing for Seed or Plumb Cake.

Take two pounds of double-refin'd ſugar pounded and ſifted; beat ſix whites of eggs to a froth; caſt a little gum-water alongſt with the eggs; then mix in the ſugar, and beat it until it is very thick; it will take two kours beating: put it on the cake when it is taken out of the oven; then put it again into the oven a little, but take care it be not too hot.

To mango Cucumbers.

Take the greeneſt and largeſt cucumbers.

bers you can get, before they begin to
turn yellow ; make a pickle of falt and
water fo ftrong as to carry an egg ; let
them lie four days in it; make a flit in
one of the creffes ; fcoop out all the
pulp; mix fome black and Jamaica pepper, according to the quantity of cucumbers; cut down three or four nutmegs ;
flice fome ginger, cloves, and fome
blades of mace ; mix all thefe with a
little muftard-feed; fill up every cucumber with thefe fpices, and put a fingle
clove of garlick into every cucumber ;
then tie them round with thread to keep
in the fpices ; lay green-kail blades in
the bottom of the pan; lay in the mangoes, and ftrew a good deal of pounded
alum over them; then put in an equal
quantity of water and vinegar, more
than will cover them ; put in along
with the alum a bit of faltpetre ; cover
them up with blades, and put them on
the fire ; give them a good hear, but
don't let them boil; take them off, and
let them ftand an hour; then put them
on again and repeat this for two or
                                    three

three times: the laſt time you put them on, let them boil until they are of a good green; then take them out of that, and lay them between the folds of two cloths, with the cut ſide undermoſt to dry ; then clean the pan, and take as much ſtrong vinegar as will cover them; put them into your pots, and pour the vinegar boiling hot upon them ; put amongſt them any of the ſpices that was left from filling them up ; cover them with two or three folds of a clean cloth until they are cold.

All green pickles are done in the ſame way as the mangoes; ſuch as ſmall cucumbers, kidney-beans, ſamphire, raddiſh pods, Indian creſſes ſeed, &c.

To pickle Walnuts.

Take full-grown walnuts before the ſhells turn hard, ſo that you can run a pin eaſily through them; prick every nut with a big pin; boil a pickle of ſalt and water ſo ſtrong as to bear an egg ; ſcum it when it boils, and pour it hot

on

on the nuts ; lay a weight on them to
hold them down, and every four days
make a new pickle as ftrong as the firft ;
continue fo doing for four or five times ;
and when you take them out of the laft
brine, rub each nut with a clean coarfe
cloth ; boil as much ftrong vinegar as
will cover them ; take black and Jamaica pepper, cloves, and mace ; cut
two or three nutmegs ; flice a piece of
ginger and a piece of horfe-radifh ;
put in three or four fpoonfuls of muftard-feed, and a few cloves of garlick ;
ftrew in the fpices amongft the walnuts
as you put them in ; then pour the vinegar boiling hot on them, and cover
them up with two or three folds of a
clean cloth.

To pickle Mufhrooms.

Take the fmall white buttons ; throw
them in milk and water ; take them out
of that, and rub every mufhroom with
a piece of clean flannel ; and as you rub
them, throw them into clean milk and
water ; then put them into a pan of
clean

clean cold water with a little bit of
alum; put them on the fire; let them
be near the boil, but not to boil; take
them off, and spread them between two
cloths to dry; have ready boil'd as
much of the strongest vinegar as will
cover them; then put the mushrooms
into bottles with whole white pepper,
cloves, mace, and ginger. The vinegar
must be quite cold before you put it on
them; put a little sweet oil on the tops
of the bottles; cork and tie them up
very close with a piece of leather.

To pickle Cauliflowers.

Take the cauliflowers when they are
no larger than a small turnip; take away
all the green leaves from them; put on
some milk and water; and when it
boils, put in the flowers, and scald them
in it; take them off, and lay them between two cloths to dry; and when
they are dry, put them into a jar: put
in whole white pepper, mace, cloves,
and a bit of ginger, amongst them; boil
as much of the best vinegar as will co-

ver

ver them; you muſt let it be cold before
you put it on them : you muſt be ſure
that the cauliflowers be hard, white, and
free of all blemiſhes. You may pickle
turnip in the ſame way, but turn them
out with a turner : if you have none,
pare and cut them down very neatly
in pieces about the ſize of a walnut.

To pickle Onions.

Take ſmall hard onions; the ſilver
onions are the beſt; put them into a pan
with cold water, put them on the fire,
and let them be very near boiling; then
take off the ſkins, and lay them between
two cloths till they are cold ; put in
white pepper, mace, cloves, and ginger,
amongſt them ; boil ſome vinegar, and
when it is cold pour it on them.

To pickle Red Cabbage.

Cut down the cabbage in very thin
ſlices, and ſtrew a good handful of ſalt
in amongſt them; preſs them down in
a can, and let them ſtand twenty-four
hours ; then ſqueeze all the juice very
well

well with your hand out of them; mix
fome black and Jamaica pepper and
cloves with the cabbage; pour vinegar
boiling hot upon them; cover up the
mouth of the can with two or three
folds of a cloth, and when they are
cold clofe them up.

To pickle Bitroot.

Put the bitroot into a pot full of boiling water; take care not to cut nor
break any of the fmall fibres nor the
fhaws: when they are boiled tender
enough, let them cool a little, and take
off the fkins with a coarfe cloth; flice
them down into a pot, and put in fome
black and Jamaica pepper and cloves
among them, and fill up the pot with
cold vinegar. If you have a mind to
dye any of the turnips or onions red,
put them in amongft the bitroot. You
may flice a few onions, and throw in a-
mongft pickled cabbage; it gives them
a good relifh.

To

To pickle Barberries.

Take equal quantity of vinegar and water; into a chopin of that put half a pound of kitchen-fugar and a little falt; then pick out the worſt of the berries; bruife them in a mortar, and put them in amongſt the liquor; boil it till it is of a fine colour; let it ſtand to cool, and then ſtrain it through a cloth; put the beſt of the barberries into a jar, and when the pickle is cold and ſettled, pour it on them.

All pickle ſhould be covered up with a wet bladder, and a piece of leather tied above; a wooden or horn ſpoon is the beſt for lifting pickles.

To make Pickle-Lillo, or Indian Pickle.

Take a pound of white ginger; let it lie one night in falt and water; ſcrape and cut it into thin ſlices, and put it in a large ſtone-jar with dry ſalt, and let it remain till the reſt of the ingredients are ready; take one pound of garlick;

peel

peel off the fkins ; falt it three days ;
then wafh it and falt it again, and let it
lie three days longer ; then wafh it, and
put it in a fieve, and dry it in the fun;
take two ounces of long pepper ; falt and
dry it, but not too much ; take' one
ounce of white muftard feed, two ounces
of turmerick root ; pound it well, and
tie it in a muflin rag, and throw in all
thefe ingredients into a well-glaz'd earth-
en jar, putting a quart of ftrong white-
wine vinegar to them, juft cold; do not
boil it ; and if at any time the liquor
dry up, add fome more vinegar ; take
the white kind of cabbages ; cut them
into quarters ; falt them three days ;
fqueeze the water from them, and dry
them in the fun : do the fame to cauliflowers and celery, only the white part
of the celery : French beans, falad, and
afparagus, fhould only lie two days, and
have a boil in falt and water, and be
dried in the fun, and thrown into the
pickle ; keep them very clofe. White
cucumber, or plumbs and apples, may
be done in like manner with this pickle.

To

To make Sugar Vinegar.

To every pint of water take half a pound of raw fugar; let it boil, and fcum it as long as the fcum rifes; put it into a barrel that will hold it; and when it is. as cold as when you put barm (yeft) to wort, foak a toaft of bread in barm, and put to it; let it ftand until it give over hiffing; then bung it; let it ftand in an equal warm place. If you make it in April, it will be ready againft the feafon of making pickles.

To make Goofeberry Vinegar.

To every pint of goofeberries allow three pints of water; the berries muft be quite ripe; bruife them with your hand; boil the water, and let it be cold, and then put it on the berries; let it ftand twenty-four hours; then ftrain it through a clean cloth. To a pint of that juice put half a pound of raw fugar; mix it well, and when the fugar is diffolved, barrel it up; it muft ftand nine or ten months at leaft. This is a very ftrong vinegar.

To

To make Ketchup.

Take the largeft mufhrooms you can get, and cut off a bit of the end that the earth fticks on; break them in fmall pieces with your hands ; as you break them, ftrew falt on them ; let them ftand twenty-four hours ; then turn them into a hair-fearce, and ftir them often in the fearce to let the juice run from them. When you have gathered all the juice you can get, run it through a flannel bag. To every pint of juice allow an ounce of black and Jamaica pepper, two nutmegs bruifed, two drops of mace, two drops of cloves, and a piece of fliced ginger ; clarify it with the whites of eggs; and when it is very clean fcummed, put in the fpices, and let it boil until it taftes very ftrong of the fpices ; when cold, bottle it up, and put the fpices into the bottles ; pour a little fweet oil into each bottle; cork them, and tie a piece of leather above the corks.

To make Walnut Ketchup.

Take the walnuts when they are full grown,

grown, before the fhell turn hard;
prick them with a pin; make a ftrong
pickle of falt and water to bear an egg;
pour it boiling hot on the walnuts, and
let them ftand for four days; take them
up, and wafh them with clean water,
and dry them with a cloth; beat them
very well in a mortar. To every hundred
walnuts put on two bottles of ftrong
ftale beer; the ftronger the beer is the
better; let it ftand ten or twelve davs
on the walnuts; then run it through a
cloth, and ftrain it hard to get all the
juice out; then run it through a flannel bag; put it on the fire; clarify it
with whites of eggs; when it is clean
fcummed, put in black and Jamaica
pepper, cloves, nutmegs, mace, fliced
ginger, horfe-radifh fliced, and a quarter of a pound of anchovies; let them
boil until they are ftrong of the fpices;
then run it through a fearce; divide the
fpices equally amongft the bottles, and
put in a fingle clove of garlick into each
bottle; when the ketchup is cold, cork
it up as the other ketchup.

To

To make a Twenty-pint Barrel of Double Rum Shrub.

Beat eighteen pounds of single refin'd sugar; put it into the barrel, and pour a pint of lemon and a pint of orange juice upon the sugar; shake the barrel often, and stir it up with a clean stick till the sugar is dissolved. Before you squeeze the fruit, pare four dozen of the lemons and oranges very thin; put on some rum on the rhind, and let it stand until it is to go into the barrel: when the sugar is all melted, fill up the barrel with the rum, and put in the rum that the rhind is amongst along with it. Before the barrel is quite full, shake it heartily, that it may be all well mix'd; then fill up the barrel with the rum, and bung it up; let it stand six weeks before you pierce it. If you see it is not fine enough, let it stand a week or two longer.

To make the true French white Ratafia, which is one of the best compounded Drams.

To two pints of brandy take four ounces of the kernels of apricots and peaches;

peaches; bruife them in the mortar;
take the thin parings of a dozen of lemons and fix oranges; bruife an ounce
of coriander feed; break half an ounce
of cinnamon in fmall bits, and take
twenty whole cloves; mix all thefe materials with the brandy. You may let
them ftand a month or fix weeks, ftirring them often; put it through a fearce,
and take a pound and a half of fine fugar; clarify it, and mix it with the
fpirits; then bottle it; put the corks
loofe in, and let it ftand until it is quite
fine; pour it from the grounds into o-
ther bottles. You may filter the grounds
through a paper or cotton in a filler.

As we have not many of thefe fruits,
bitter almonds will fupply their place;
but take only the half of the quantity,
and don't bruife them, but cut them
fmall with a knife. You may put on a
pint of good whifky on the materials,
and put a good piece of fugar in it. It
is a good feafoning for puddings, or a
common dram.

PILLS

BILLS of FARE.

•••{•••{••••{••{•••{••{•••{•

Family Dinners of Five Diſhes.

	Soup.	
Potatoes.	Plum-pudding. Roaſt Beef.	Pickles.

••{••{••{••{••{••{••{•

	Dreſt Lamb's head.	
Kidney Beans.	Baked Pudding. Roaſt Mntton.	Sliced Cucumber.

••{••{••{••{••{••{••{•

	Boiled Haddocks, or Fiſh in ſeaſon.	
Brocoli.	Baked Pudding. Roaſt Veal.	Pickles.

••{••{••{••{••{••{••{•

	Boiled Pork.	
Greens.	Soup. Roaſt Turkey.	Peaſe Pudding.

••{••{••{••{••{••{••{•

	Stewed Tongue.	
Spinage.	Boiled Pudding. Roaſt Rabbits.	Cauliflower.

••{••{••{••{••{••{••{•

	Hancot of Mutton.	
Peas.	Baked Pudding. Roaſt Gooſe.	Apple ſauce.

M   A

Apple
Sauce.

A Small Cod.
Beef Steak Pie.

Roast Pork.

Fish
Sauce.

><+<+<+<+<+<+<+<+<+<+<+<><

Pease.

A Round of Beef
and Carrots.
Boiled Pudding.
Roast Lamb.

Salad.

Family Dinners of Seven Dishes.

Egg Sauce.

Salad.

Tusk Fish.

Soup.

Roast Loin
of Veal.

Potatoes.

Cheese-cakes.

><+<+<+<+<+<+<+<+<+<+<+<><

Scolloped
Oysters.

Brocoli.

Drest Calf's Head.

Apple Pie.

Boiled Beef
and Greens.

Asparagus.

Fretters.

><+<+<+<+<+<+<+<+<+<+<+<><

Almond
Cheese-cakes.

Ratafia
Cream.

Stewed Rump
of Beef.

Floating Island.

Roast Turkey.

Lemon
Cream.

Confection
Tarts.

Stewed	Jagged Hare.	Cuſtard
Celery.		Pudding.
	Pickles.	
Tarts.		Potatoes.
	Saddle of Mutton.	

Family Dinners of Eight Diſhes.

Cod's Head removed, with
Roaſted Duckling.

Gooseberry		Fricaſee
Sauce.		of Pallets.
	Orange Pudding.	
Minched Pies		Cauliflower.
	Boiled Leg Lamb and Loin fried.	

Soup removed,
Roaſt Pig.

Fricaſee		Lemon
Whitens.		Pudding.
	Cuſtard in Cups.	
Cold Tongue.		Maſh'd Turnip
	Boiled Leg Mutton, Cauper Sauce.	

Family Dinner of Nine Diſhes.

Fiſh removed,
Ragoo of Pigeons.

Lemon		Fricaſee
Pudding.		of Kernels.
Bacon and Beans.	Soup.	Boiled Chickens.
Cauliflower.		Pickles.
	Roaſted Beef.	

M 2

Family Dinner of Ten Dishes.

Salmon removed,
Roast Turkey.

Stewed Cellery.

Marrow pasty.

Veal Cutlets.

Soup.

Fried Fish.
Fine baked
Pudding.
Sliced Turnips and
Carrot, with melted
Butter over them.

Boiled Tongue
and Udder with Roots.

Family Dinner of Twelve Dishes.

Soup removed, with
Boiled Mutton and
Cauper Sauce.

Boiled Chickens
with Cream Sauce.
Stewed
Mushrooms.

Lobster.

Cheese-cakes.

Pigeon Pie.
Confection Tarts.
Roast Hare.

Roast
Tongue.
Artichoke Bottoms Fricasee.

Veal Olives.

Family Dinner of Fifteen Dishes.

Soup removed,
Boiled Turkey with
Oyster Sauce.

Stewed Peas
and Lettuce.

Ratafia Cream.
Apricot Tart.
Blanc-mange.
Fricasee.

Hen's Nest.

Syllabubs.
Jelly in a Cheap.

Roast Pig.

Scotch
Collops.

Rasberry Cream.
Orange Pudding.
Egg Cheese.
Wild Fowls.

THINGS FOR SUPPER-DISHES.

Minced veal—Beef fteaks—Roaft fowl, chicken, duck, hot or cold—Roaft hare—Cold fliced beef, cold ham, cold tongue—Scollop oyfters or pickled oyf-ters—Boiled tripe—Broiled fifh—Sau-fages, rafped beef—any fort of potted meat—Veal cutlets, Scotch collops, cold veal or mutton hafhed—Fricafee of chicken, veal, lamb kernels, or any white meat—Pigeons roafted or broiled —Giblets ftewed—Sliced coler—Lob-fter, anchovies, and fliced butter—Salmagundy—Turkey pout roafted, or any kind of wild-fowl roafted—Cold wild-fowl or hare ftewed down—Pickles—Fine minced pies, tarts, cheefe-cakes, fine baked pudding, fritters, German puffs—Blanc-mange, trifle, or any fort of creams you choofe—Spinage, af-paragus, peas, artichokes, falad—Potch-ed eggs and forrel—Celery ftewed or for a falad—Potatoes. Have always fome garden difhes according to the feafons at fupper. Buttered crabs in the fhell, com-monly called *parton pies*—Pan-cakes.

A

A
LIST
OF
THINGS IN SEASON,
IN EVERY MONTH OF THE YEAR.

JANUARY.

Meat.
House Lamb,
Pork,
Beef,
Mutton,
Veal.

Fish.
Haddocks,
Cod,
Soles,
Turbot,
Thornback,
Skate,
Whitings,
Smelts,
Carp,
Tench,
Perch,
Eels,
Lampreys,
Plaice,
Flounders,

Lobsters,
Crabs,
Cray-Fish,
Prawns,
Oyfters,
Sturgeon.

Poultry.
Hare,
Pheafant,
Partridge,
Woodcocks,
Snipes,
Turkeys,
Capons,
Pullets,
Fowls,
Chickens,
Tame Pigeons,
Rabbts.

Vegetables.
Cabbage,
Savoys,

Coleworts,
Sprouts,
Borecole,
Brocoli, purple
and white,
Spinage,
Cardoons,
Parfnips,
Carrots,
Turnips,
Celery,
Endive,
Leeks,
Onions,
Potatoes,
Beets,
Garlick,
Efchalot,
Mufhrooms,
Saltafy,
Scorzonera,
Skurrets,

Sorrel,
Burnet,
Parfley,
Sage,
Thyme,
Rofemary,
Lettuce,
Creffes,
Muftard,
Rape,
Radifh,
Taragon,
Mint,
Chervil.

Fruit.
Apples,
Pears,
Nuts,
Almonds,
Services,
Medlars,
Grapes.

FEBRUARY.

FEBRUARY.

Meat.
House Lamb,
Pork,
Beef,
Mutton,
Veal.

Fish.
Haddocks,
Cod,
Soles,
Turbot,
Thornback,
Skate,
Whitings.
Smelts,
Carp,
Tench,
Perch,
Eels,
Lampreys,
Plaice,
Flounders,

Lobsters,
Crabs,
Cray-fish,
Prawns,
Oysters,
Sturgeon.

Poultry.
Hare,
Pheasant,
Partridge,
Woodcock,
Snipes,
Turkeys,
Capons,
Pullets,
Fowls,
Chickens,
Pigeons,
Tame Rabbits.

Vegetables.
Cabbage,
Savoys,

Coleworts,
Sprouts,
Borecole,
Brocoli, purple
and white,
Cardoons,
Spinage,
Carrots,
Parsnips,
Turnips,
Celery,
Endive,
Leeks,
Onions,
Potatoes,
Beets,
Garlic,
Eschalot,
Mushrooms,
Salsify,
Scorzonera,
Skirrets,

Sorrel,
Burnet,
Parsley,
Thyme,
Winter Savoury,
Rosemary,
Sage,
Marigold,
Lettuce,
Cresses,
Mustard,
Rape,
Radish,
Taragon,
Mint,
Chervil,
Jerusalem Artichokes.

Fruit.
Apples,
Pears.

MARCH.

Meat.
House Lamb,
Pork,
Beef,
Mutton,
Veal.

Fish.
Turbot,
Soles,
Thornback,
Skate,
Whitings,
Carp,
Tench,
Eels,
Plaice,

Flounders,
Mullets,
Lobsters,
Crabs,
Cray-fish,
Prawns.

Poultry.
Turkeys,
Capons,
Pullets,
Fowls,
Chickens,
Pigeons,
Ducklings,
Tame Rabbits.

Vegetables.
Cabbage,
Savoys,
Coleworts,
Sprouts,
Borecole,
Brocoli, Purple
and White,
Spinage,
Cardoons,
Parsnips,
Carrots,
Turnips,
Celery,
Endive,
Onions,

Potatoes,
Beets,
Garlic,
Eschalot,
Mushrooms,
Burnet,
Parsley,
Thyme,
Savoury,
Rosemary,
Sage,
Sorrel,
Marigolds,
Lettuce,
Cresses,
Mustard,

Rape.

Rape,	Chervil,	Tanfy,	*Fruit.*
Radifh,	Jerufalem Arti-	Cucumbers,	Pears,
Taragon,	chokes,	Afparagus,	Apples.
Mint,	Celery,	Purflane.	

A P R I L.

Meat.	Chubs,	*Vegetables.*	Beet,
GRafs Lamb,	Mullets,	Coleworts,	Lettuce,
Beef,	Cray-fifh,	Sprouts,	All forts of fmall
Mutton,	Crabs,	Young Carrots,	Salad,
Veal.	Lobfters,	Brocoli,	All forts of Pot
Fifh.	Prawns.	Spinage,	Herbs,
Turbot,		Parfley,	Young fhoots of
Soles,	*Poultry.*	Chervil,	Saliafy,
Skate,	Leverets,	Young Onions,	Cucumbers,
Carp,	Rabbits,	Celery,	Tragopogon.
Tench,	Ducklings,	Endive,	
Trout,	Pigeons,	Sorrel,	*Fruit.*
Herring,	Pullets,	Burnet,	Pears,
Salmon,	Fowls,	Radifhes,	Apples.
Smelts,	Chickens,	Afparagus,	

M A Y.

	Herrings,		All forts of falad,
	Eels,	*Vegetables.*	All forts of herbs,
Meat.	Chub,	Cabbages,	Peafe,
	Lobfter,	Potatoes,	Beans,
LAmb,	Cray-fifh,	Carrots,	Afparagus,
Beef,	Crabs,	Turnips,	Tragopogon,
Mutton,	Prawns.	Caulilower	Cucumbers.
Veal.		Artichokes,	
	Poultry	Radifhes,	*Fruit.*
Fifh.		Spinage,	Apples,
Turbot,	Green Geefe,	Parfley,	Pears,
Carp,	Ducklings,	Sorrel,	Cherries,
Tench,	Leverets,	Balm,	Some Strawber-
Trout,	Rabbits,	Mint,	ries,
Salmon,	Pullets,	Purflane,	Goofeberries and
Soles,	Fowls,	Fennel,	Currants for
Smelts,	Chickens,	Lettuce,	Tarts.

JUNE.

JUNE.

Meat.
LAMB,
Beef,
Mutton,
Veal,
Buck Venison.

Fish.
Turbot,
Mackerel,
Trout,
Carp,
Tench,
Pike,
Salmon,
Soles,

Herrings,
Smelts,
Eels,
Mullets,
Lobsters,
Cray-fish,
Prawns.

Poultry.
Green Geese,
Ducklings,
Turkey Poults,
Plovers,
Wheat Ears,
Leverets,
Rabbits,

Fowls,
Pullets,
Chickens.

Vegetables.
Cucumbers,
Pease,
Beans,
Kidney Beans,
Asparagus,
Cabbages,
Cauliflowers,
Artichokes,
Carrots,
Turnips,
Potatoes,

Radishes,
Onions,
Lettuce,
All small Sallad,
All Pot Herbs,
Parsley,
Purslane.

Fruit.
Strawberries,
Cherries,
Currants,
Gooseberries,
Apricots,
Apples,
Pears.

JULY.

Meat.
LAMB,
Beef,
Mutton,
Veal,
Buck Venison.

Fish.
Cod,
Haddock,
Mackerel,
Soles,
Herrings,
Salmon,
Carp,
Tench,
Plaice,
Mullet,
Flounders,

Skate,
Thornback,
Pike,
Eels,
Lobsters,
Prawns,
Cray-fish,

Poultry.
Green Geese,
Ducklings,
Turkey Poults,
Leverets,
Rabbits,
White Ears,
Plovers,
Pigeons,
Pullets,
Fowls,
Chickens.

Vegetables.
Pease,
Beans,
Kidney Beans,
Cabbage,
Cauliflower,
Cucumbers,
Mushrooms,
Carrots,
Turnips,
Potatoes,
Radishes,
Finochia,
Scorzonera,
Salsafy,
Artichokes,
Celery,
Endive,
Chervil,

Sorrel,
Purslane,
Parsley,
All sorts of Sallad,
All sorts of Pot Herbs.

Fruits.
Pears,
Apples,
Cherries,
Strawberries,
Rasberries,
Peaches,
Nectarines,
Plums,
Apricots,
Gooseberries,
Melons.

AUGUST.

Meat.
LAMB,
Beef,

Mutton,
Veal,
Buck Venison.

Fish.
Cod,

Haddocks,
Mackarel,
Herring,
Skate,

Skate,	Wild Ducks,	Mushrooms,	All forts of Sallad,
Plaice,	Pullet,	Sprouts,	All forts of Herbs
Flounders,	Fowls,	Carrots,	Dill,
Thornback,	Chickens.	Turnips,	Spinage.
Mullet,	Leverets,	Potatoes,	
Pike,	Rabbits,	Radifhes,	*Fruit.*
Carp,	Pigeons,	Finochia,	Pears,
Eels,	Plovers,	Scorzonera,	Apples,
Oyfters,	Pheafant,	Salfafy,	Peaches,
Lobfters,	Wheat Ears.	Onions,	Nectarines,
Cray-fifh,		Garlic,	Plums,
Prawns.	*Vegetables.*	Efchalot,	Grapes,
	Peafe,	Artichokes,	Figs,
Poultry.	Beans,	Celery,	Filberts,
Moor Game,	Kidney Beans,	Endive,	Mulberries,
Turkey Poults,	Cabbage,	Sorrel,	Goofeberries,
Geefe,	Cauliflower,	Parfley,	Currants,
Ducks,	Cucumbers,	Purflane,	Melons.

SEPTEMBER.

Meat.	Lobfters.	Kidney Beans,	Finochia,
LAMB,		Cauliflower,	Lettuce, and all
Beef,	*Poultry.*	Cabbage,	forts of Salad,
Mutton,	Geefe,	Sprouts,	All forts of Herbs
Veal,	Turkics,	Carrots,	Radifhes.
Buck Venifon.	Pullets,	Turnips,	*Fruit.*
	Fowls,	Parfnips,	Currants,
Fifh.	Chickens,	Potatoes,	Plums,
Cod,	Ducks,	Artichokes,	Peaches,
Haddock,	Pigeons,	Cucumbers,	Pears.
Salmon,	Rabbits,	Mufhrooms,	Apples,
Carp,	Teal,	Efchalots,	Grapes,
Tench,	Larks,	Onions,	Figs,
Plaice,	Hares,	Leeks,	Walnuts,
Flounders,	Pheafant,	Garlic,	Filberts,
Thornback,	Partridge,	Scorzonera,	Hazle Nuts,
Skate,	Moor Game.	Salfafy,	Medlars,
Soles,		Cardoons,	Quinces,
Smelts,	*Vegetables.*	Endive,	Lazaroles,
Pike,	Peafe,	Celery,	Cherries,
Oyfters,	Beans,	Parfley,	Melons.

OCTOBER.

OCTOBER.

Meat.
PORK,
  Lamb,
Mutton,
Beef,
Veal.
Doe Venison.
   Fish.
Salmon Trout,
Smelts,
Carp,
Tench,
Doree,
Berbet,
Holobet,
Brills,
Gudgeons,
Pike,
Perch,
Lobsters,
Oysters,
Muscles,

Cockles,

   Poultry.
Turkeys,
Geese,
Pigeons,
Pullets,
Fowls,
Chickens,
Wild-Ducks,
Teal,
Widgeon,
Larks,
Woodcock,
Snipes,
Hares,
Pheasants,
Partridges,
Dotterels,
Rabbits.
   Vegetables.
Cabbage,

Cauliflower,
Brocoli,
Savoys,
Sprouts,
Colewort,
Carrots,
Turnips,
Potatoes,
Parsnips,
Skirrets,
Salsafy,
Scorzonera,
Turnip-rooted
  and Black Spa-
   nish Radish,
Some Artichokes
Onions,
Leeks,
Eschalot,
Rocombole,
Celery,
Endive,

Chard Beets,
Beets,
Finochia,
Chervil,
Mushrooms,
Lettuce & small
  Salad,
All sorts of
  Herbs.
   Fruit.
Pears,
Apples,
Peaches,
Figs,
Medlars,
Services,
Quinces,
Bullace,
Grapes,
Walnuts,
Filberts,
Nuts.

NOVEMBER.

Meat.
HOuse Lamb,
  Pork,
Beef,
Mutton,
Veal.

   Fish.
Salmon,
Salmon Trout,
Carp,
Tench,
Pike,
Gurnet,
Doree.
Holobet,
Berbet,
Smelts,

Gudgeons,
Lobsters,
Oysters,
Cockles,
Muscles.
   Poultry.
Turkeys,
Geese,
Fowls,
Pullets,
Chickens,
Pigeons,
Wild-Ducks,
Teal,
Widgeon,
Woodcocks,
Snipes,
Larks,

Dotterels.
Hares,
Pheasants,
Partridges,
Rabbits.
   Vegetables.
Cabbage,
Savoys,
Borecole,
Sprouts,
Colewort,
Cauliflower,
Spinage,
Jerusalem Arti-
  chokes,
Carrots,
Turnips,
Parsnips,

Potatoes,
Salsafy,
Skirrets,
Scorzonera,
Onions,
Leeks,
Eschalot,
Rocombole,
Beet,
Chard Beet,
Cardoons,
Parsley,
Celery,
Cresses,
Endive,
Chervil,
Lettuce and small
  Sallad

All sorts of Herbs Apples, Hazle Nuts, Services,
  Fruit. Bullace, Walnuts, Grapes.
Pears, Chesnuts, Medlars,

DECEMBER.

Meat.
HOuse Lamb, Pork,
Beef,
Mutton,
Veal,
Doe Venison.

Fish.
Haddocks,
Cod,
Codlings,
Soles,
Carp,
Smelts,
Gurnets,
Sturgeon,
Dorees,
Holobets,
Berbet,
Gudgeons,

Eels,
Oysters,
Cockles,
Muscles.

Poultry.
Turkies,
Geese,
Pullets,
Capons,
Fowls,
Chickens,
Pigeons,
Rabbits,
Woodcocks,
Snipes,
Hares,
Partridges,
Pheasant,
Teal,

Widgeon,
Dotterels,
Larks,
Wild Ducks.

Vegetables.
Purple and white Brocoli,
Cabbages,
Savoys,
Borecole,
Carrots,
Parsnips,
Turnips,
Potatoes,
Skirrets.
Scorzonera,
Salsafy,
Leeks,
Onions,

Eschalot,
Rocombole,
Celery,
Endive,
Spinage,
Beets,
Cresses,
Lettuce and small
 Sallad,
Pot Herbs,
Cardoons.

Fruit.
Apples,
Pears,
Medlars,
Services,
Chesnuts,
Grapes.

F I N I S.

You may also be interested in these titles:

Townsends is please to make available a growing list of rare and valuable books from the 18th and early 19th centuries, including those listed below. Be sure to visit our website for a complete list of titles.

Cookbooks

The Art of Cookery by Hannah Glasse (1765)

The Domestick Coffee-Man by Humphrey Broadbent (1722) and *The New Art of Brewing Beer* by Thomas Tyron (1690)

The Complete Housewife by Eliza Smith (1730)

The Universal Cook by John Townshend (1773)

The Practice of Cookery by Mrs. Frazer (1791 & 1795)

The London Art of Cookery by John Farley (1787)

The Complete Confectioner by Hannah Glasse (1765)

A New and Easy Method of Cookery by Elizabeth Cleland (1755)

The English Art of Cookery by Richard Briggs (1788)

18th & Early 19th-Century Brewing by multiple authors

The Lady's Assistant by Charlotte Mason (1777)

The Experienced English Housekeeper by Elizabeth Raffald (1769)

The Professed Cook by B. Clermont (1769)

The Cook's and Confectioner's Dictionary by John Nott (1723)

The Modern Art of Cookery Improved by Ann Shackleford (1765)

The Country Housewife's Family Companion by William Ellis (1750)

A Collection of Above Three Hundred Receipts by Mary Kettelby (1714)

England's Newest Way in All Sorts of Cookery by Henry Howard (1726)

The Universal Cook by Francis Collingwood & John Woollams (1792)

The Court and Country Cook by Massialot (1702)

Professed Cookery by Ann Cook (1760)

—*⁄⁄⁄⁄※⁄⁄⁄⁄*—

Biographies & Journals

The Hessians by multiple authors

*Travels Through the Interior Parts of North-America
in the Years 1766, 1767, and 1768* by Jonathan Carver (1778)

The Women of the American Revolution, Volumes 1, 2, & 3
by Elizabeth Ellet (1848)

The Backwoods of Canada by Catharine Parr Traill (1836)

Travels into North America by Peter Kalm (1760)

New Travels in the United States of America. Performed in 1788
and *The Commerce of America and Europe*
by J.P. Brissot De Warville (1792 & 1795)

The Journal of Nicholas Cresswell, 1774–1777
by Nicholas Cresswell (1924)

An Account of the Life of the Late Reverend Mr. David Brainerd
by Jonathan Edwards (1765 & 1824)

*Travels for Four Years and a Half in the United States of America
During 1798, 1799, 1800, 1801, and 1802* by John Davis (1909)

*Travels through North and South Carolina, Georgia,
East and West Florida* by William Bartram (1792)

A Tour in the United States of America, Volumes 1 & 2
by John F. Smyth Stuart (1784)

Simcoe's Military Journal
by J. G. Simcoe (1844)

Townsends

www.townsends.us

Made in the USA
Las Vegas, NV
23 May 2022

49266641R00154